DOGS

DOGS

101 ANSWERS TO COMMONLY ASKED QUESTIONS

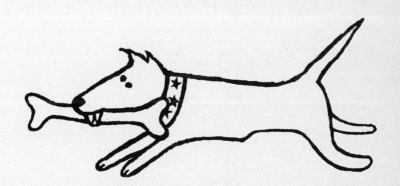

DR ROB ZAMMIT

A Sue Hines Book
Allen & Unwin

For my wife, Fiona, whose patient smiles and shakes of the head warm my heart, even though my professional activities continue to ruin so many of her dinner parties.

First published in Australia in 2002

A Sue Hines Book
Allen & Unwin
83 Alexander Street
Crows Nest NSW 2065
Australia
Phone: (61 2) 8425 0100
Fax: (61 2) 9906 2218
Email: info@allenandunwin.com
Web: www.allenandunwin.com

National Library of Australia
Cataloguing-in-Publication entry:

Zammit, Robert.
 Dogs : 101 answers to commonly asked questions about dogs.
 ISBN 1 86508 879 X.
 1. Dogs. I. Title.
 636.7

Designed by Andrew Cunningham, Studio Pazzo
Cover photographs of author by Michael Kennedy
Cover photograph of dog by Cabal Canine Candids
Typeset by Pauline Haas

Printed by McPherson's Printing Group

Contents

Hey doc, about my dog ...

A strong wind is blowing in from the bay so I clutch my child close, shielding her from the cold. I love this moment because we live so far from the sea, so I close my eyes, turn my face to the wind and inhale deeply, and I swear I can taste the salt carried in the air. Suddenly the quiet moment is interrupted by a stranger's voice, 'I know who you are, but don't worry I won't interrupt you'. The lady has recognised me from recent television appearances. Then she goes on to say, 'Can I ask you just a quick question about my dog?' I really don't mind these interruptions, and they happen all the time. I live, eat and sleep dogs and I get a good feeling from helping people out.

There's never been a time in my life without dogs. As a child, my school tie was handy for bringing home any strays that congregated at the train station. Having witnessed one dog torn apart by a passing train, I feared for their lives. My tie around a dog's neck would encourage it home to a feed and safety, much to the groans of consternation from my parents.

Dogs bring us much happiness. Good health has been linked to dog ownership, too, with scientific evidence pointing to the fact that people who own dogs are more likely to have lower blood pressure and fewer heart attacks. However, caring for a dog can be complex, with all those decisions be made about the type of dog, the level of veterinary care, what to feed it, how and when to training it and whether or not you need advice from a behavioural specialist.

Over the years I've learnt much about the care of dogs. And I'm a very lucky man because I love my work and I love helping and teaching people about animals. This book is an extension of the buzz I get from telling someone how they can help their dog. Hopefully it will help you and one of the loves of your life.

1. How do I select the right breed of dog?

So many people select a dog simply because of a single feature that attracts them to the breed, or because they've wanted one since they were a child. The problem with this approach is that it's not very well thought out. Yet that's what happens: as children, many of us fall in love with a breed of dog because we see them on television or have some other association with them, then decide we have to have one, without thinking the whole commitment through.

I see the result of these kinds of decisions every day. I'll give you an example. A friend wanted to buy a West Highland white terrier and asked if I thought it would suit her. She was a very busy person with two young children and a beautiful, well-kept garden in her backyard. My answer had to be no. The advice was ignored and very soon after the purchase, my friend was on the phone again for help. The initial problem was that the dog was biting the kids (in play), and then barking and digging and destroying anything in the back-yard were added to the list. Finally, the kids refused to go outside to play because the dog was over-exuberant, so she had to find a new home for the animal.

In this case, my friend wanted the pup because of how cute the dogs look; she had not really taken into consideration the breed's characteristic determined, wilful temperament. She had ignored the time required to train the pup and the effort needed for proper socialisation. Educating the pup into accepting rules about the household never happened, so disaster beckoned.

For lots of reasons, it is hard to choose the right dog. No species, including those that are now extinct, has had as much variation as dogs, *Canis familiaris*. From the tiny chihuahua through to the largest of canines, the Irish wolfhound, the variation means not only many different shapes but also many different needs. The wide range of breeds available makes it that much more difficult for prospective owners to select the right breed. On top of that, the choices have further widened now that we travel more, and new breeds are being introduced into areas where they were previously unavailable. Alaskan Malamutes have become popular in regions with warm climates while the desert dogs of Arabia, the Salukis, can now be found throughout every continent.

Remember that when humans select the wrong breed, it's usually the dog that suffers. Abandoned or totally confined, never being allowed proper social interaction with people or other animals, an unloved dog may become an anti-social creature, fearful and ready to bite anyone that approaches.

So how do we choose the right breed?

The oldest rule says that the breed you choose should relate to the size of your backyard. People believed they required a big backyard to house a big breed. Yet, many a large dog can find comfortable housing in a town house or apartment, providing the owners are sufficiently committed to caring for the dog. In fact, there are many cases of people with small dogs in large, roomy areas that fail to care for the dog properly because the breed is too active, too hairy or there is some other reason for non-compatibility between human and dog.

The most important rule in selecting a breed of dog is that the breed you choose has to suit your commitment to your dog; that is, how much time and money you are prepared to spend on your animal. Also, and this is an extremely difficult thing to do, you need to examine your own personality. If you have a soft or meek personality, not really assertive, you would do well to avoid dominant breeds such as Rottweilers, German shepherds, Akitas, Dobermans and the like.

Likewise, if you tend to be flamboyant and a bit of an extrovert, then a more sedate breed may not suit you. In fact, such people can cause a dog such as the smaller toy breeds or many of the hounds, to become shy. And a shy dog is usually the most dangerous as it may become a dog that bites out of fear. Dominant humans who do not take time to understand dogs can inflict problems upon their pets, often with some degree of cruelty. 'They need a firm hand' or 'You need to hit them every now and then' are common statements about dogs, made by overbearing owners who have no understanding of dog training or psychology.

One of the fastest growing specialist areas in the animal profession at the moment is that of the behavioural specialist who manages problem dogs. Oddly enough, the specialists are often attempting to train the owners, rather than working on the dogs themselves. A good one will require dog owners to make some changes in the way they are treating their pet. They tell owners that they are trying to modify the dog's behaviour while they are actually modifying the owner's behaviour! The dog's response is always borne within; it was just waiting for the right signal from its pack leader, the owner.

Exercise plays a crucial role in breed selection but not just in relation to the size of your yard. A dog doesn't exercise itself because it has a large backyard; dogs simply do not put callisthenics on their daily agenda. Yard size is not the all-important factor; rather it's Grandfather Time. This is especially true these days when some people can't find the time to take their dog out for the proper exercise it needs. Suitable exercise should not only afford a dog the physical exertion it requires to stay fit but must also provide much needed mental stimulation. The sights and smells the dog comes into contact with on a walk provide much greater mental stimulation than sitting in a dreary backyard every day.

And as if all that is not enough, you need to consider such issues as annual holidays or even an overnight stay away from home. Who will look after the family pooch when everyone is away on holidays? Remember, your responsibilities to your dog aren't just placed on hold when it suits you. Boarding or arranging someone reliable to live in can be expensive but it is essential. It's better to consider these things before you buy a dog rather than see it suffer because you no longer have time to devote to its proper care.

Analyse this to pick a suitable breed of dog:

1   Do you promise to walk the dog at least five times each week?
2   Will you attend obedience classes on a regular basis for at least six months?
3   In your family, is there anyone who is scared of dogs?
4   Does your household budget stretch enough to feed another mouth?
5   Do you know where your dog will spend your holidays?
6   Can you afford veterinary fees, such as de-sexing?
7   Will you brush your dog at least once a week?
8   Do you promise to take your dog to the vet for annual vaccinations?
9   Will you remember to worm your dog regularly?
10 Can you dispose of the dog's droppings in a suitable fashion, keeping your yard clean and not affecting the environment?
11 Can you provide suitable bedding and an appropriate yard to confine your dog?
12 Are you prepared for a ten to fourteen year commitment?

If you answer no to four or more questions then a stuffed toy may be more appropriate than a live dog.

No to the first three questions means you should consider buying a small, more sedate breed of dog such as a Cavalier King Charles spaniel or a French bulldog.

No to question 2 means you are unable to commit to training a dog, so forget the dominant breeds. Regardless of your personality, a dominant breed such as a Rottweiler, Doberman, Akita, Alaskan Malamute, German shepherd or the like, need, or rather deserve, formal training.

No to question 7 means that you need to avoid any hairy breeds. Low maintenance will be your go so get a short-coated breed. Remember, though, that grooming is vital for all dogs.

2. What's your favourite breed?

I've owned dogs all my life, have loved them all, and they have more than returned that love. When I was fifteen years old a special dog entered my life and saw me through all those difficult adolescent years. Strauss, a German shepherd, was one of the reasons I became a vet and I spent many years searching for another dog like him. What I've since learnt is that it's individual dogs that are special and not a particular breed.

You can tell which is the largest or smallest, hairiest or baldest, quietest or liveliest, even friendliest or most aloof, but you can never predict when that special friend will come along. But I can say, given the right environment and opportunity, every dog, regardless of breed, will love you beyond life itself.

Having said that, knowing definite characteristics that are inherent to a particular breed can allow a family or individual to purchase a dog that will suit their needs for the next ten to fifteen years. So here are some of my favourite breeds, though I do have many more . . .

Australian shepherd

Now I'm not including this breed just to be patriotic; in fact, the Australian shepherd was developed in the United States of America! A very instinctive working dog around sheep or cattle, the breed is said to be derived from stock sent over with a load of Merinos from Australia to the USA at the turn of the nineteenth century.

The Aussie Shepherd is a medium-size-dog and they come in a multitude of colours including pure black, red, merle (mottled bluish grey), all with or without white, and with or without tan (copper) markings.

This dog is growing rapidly in popularity because of its soft dependable nature. Being so lithe on their feet and naturally gentle, they manage to play with children of all ages without ever pushing them over. Stories of them protecting children from swimming pools, busy roads and dubious strangers are commonplace to this most unassuming of canines. They're not aggressive guard-dogs by any means, but they are calmly territorial so they'll protect your property dutifully, without incessant barking. Despite their exuberance for play they take their work seriously.

They need reasonable exercise in the form of a daily walk and I've never met one yet that can't be quickly taught to retrieve a ball so this can be used to release any energy store while keeping your Aussie fit. If you really get into it, these dogs are fabulous as sports dogs, performing well at obedience trials and posting some unbelievable times in agility contests.

Coat length appears longer than a short-coated dog but they take little to look after. A wash-and-wear dog, the Aussie cleans up with a quick bath or even a brisk rub-down and brush if the weather is inclement.

Hereditary diseases have been aggressively addressed by the serious breeders who continue to test for hip dysplasia, eye defects and congenital heart defects. Be warned, the breed is sharply rising in popularity so there are some dog producers (rather than dedicated breeders) now manufacturing litters on mass rather than breeding sound stock. Remember, an honest breeder will show you clearance certificates for the parents while also offering a written guarantee.

Bichon Frise

The Bichon Frise loves to be the centre of attention and its soft expression, warm, loving eyes and gentle manners make it a dog that is easy to love. A gregarious small dog, it enjoys a good walk with its owner, where it displays its typically pretentious gait. The Bichon is highly intelligent and can become a well-mannered family member provided you don't treat it as a toy.

Give them many different experiences as youngsters: introduce them to many people and other animals, give them a few months of weekly obedience lessons and you may find you'll never want to be without a Bichon. Allow poor socialisation to dominate a Bichon pup, along with incorrect conditioning, and you may never want to inflict a Bichon on yourself again. They are all born as potential saints but reared incorrectly, they become fallen angels. The Bichon is only suitable to a committed, responsible dog owner.

Allowed to rule the house, they become difficult to toilet-train and may also develop as a nuisance barker. They can be wilful and will always test any attempt at training but persistence pays with a Bichon.

The coat of the Bichon requires clipping every six to nine weeks along with regular brushing. If you brush them daily for just a few minutes the coat remains powder-puff fluffy.

Having been bred as a walking dog, the Bichon is one of the soundest members of the toy group. They enjoy a brisk daily work-out, either a free-run in a park or a long walk on a lead. Occasionally dislocating kneecap (luxating patella) does occur but it is not common. Unfortunately, your vet cannot always tell you if a pup is going to suffer from this condition before you finalise a purchase. Dogs that develop this condition must not be used for breeding and could well require major surgery to avoid arthritis developing in the affected knee.

A Mediterranean man-about-town, the Bichon's bouncy stride, irresistible expression and soft fluffy appearance all add up to a great family pet provided you make the commitment to correct rearing.

Boxer

When it comes to dogs having a sense of humour, the boxer is notorious, often dubbed the 'clown of the dog world'. The muscular appearance exudes the dog's energetic nature — just standing still a boxer gives the appearance of an athlete: not an ounce of excess fat; sleek, firm muscles; and that slight quiver of tension, ready for take off. This lively breed is innately friendly, self-assured, fearless but never militant.

To successfully train a boxer you need to think like one. Playtime is a strong motivating factor, so utilise this as a reward to a short but successful training period. The boxer can make a top obedience dog, ensuring hours of fun at agility or obedience functions or, alternatively, it can make one of the best family dogs you can imagine. They are ready to be at your side for a long run or to be included in any backyard game or to simply laze around the house watching television. Regardless of what you ask of them, boxers will always be loyal guardians.

The very short coat makes the boxer a low maintenance pet requiring little brushing. A fastidiously clean dog that is easy to house-train, it prefers to toilet in one area of the yard rather than spreading the mess everywhere, providing of course you keep that area clean by picking up any droppings immediately.

They are very sound of limb with few hereditary joint problems; however, they can suffer from a congenital heart defect so puppies should be thoroughly checked prior to purchase. Have the breeder give you a written guarantee that they will refund you fully if the pup develops a heart defect in the first six months of life. Also ask your own vet to check the animal over within a week from purchase.

Undoubtedly the worse thing about boxers is their propensity to develop cancer; just about every type of cancer known has been seen in this breed, in particular malignant mast cell tumours and cancer of the lymphatic system. Sadly, it is not something that is currently preventable but the study of gene mapping may give invaluable insight to the genetic predispositions that lead to various cancers.

Cavalier King Charles spaniel

The Cavalier King Charles spaniel was created in the nineteenth century, its origins going back to the King Charles Spaniel which was kept by Charles I and absolutely worshipped by Charles II of England. The development of the Cavalier King Charles spaniel saw changes that gave this new breed a reputation for being a sturdy, active dog, which still had the merry but loyal attributes credited to its ancestral breed.

Cavaliers today are extremely suitable to housing with smaller yards, their demeanour making them especially attractive as a breed for young children or a companion of unfailing devotion for elderly people. But never underestimate this half-pint, ever-smiley breed: they are fantastically intelligent and enjoy the challenge and rigours of obedience training and performance.

Breeders of Cavaliers are well aware of various congenital defects and should have their stock checked for problems before they enter the animal into their breeding program. In particular the knees of a Cavalier would be checked for a condition where the kneecap dislocates out and back into position (known as luxating patella). Such a problem usually results in osteoarthritis, eventually crippling the dog in the hind legs. Eye problems can occur, so make sure the breeder has certificates from a specialist ophthalmologist, clearing both parents of any defects. Finally, the breeder should give you a money-back guarantee that your pup does not have any congenital heart defects, nor will develop any during the first year of life.

The Cavalier's coat is essentially short over the body but with some 'feathering' (long coated areas) around the ears, back of the legs, chest and tail. This longer coat needs some combing to keep it matt-free while the remainder may be brushed. Once or twice weekly will be sufficient to ensure a clean coat, healthy skin and allow the Cavalier to be free of any excess pungent, doggy smells.

The Cavalier is considered relatively strong and playful, with a sense of humour that allows it to join in any family fun. They are a wonderful introduction to the world of dogs and these canine ambassadors will quickly gain entry into your heart.

German shepherd

This breed's versatility has seen its use in every aspect where canine endeavour can make human life easier: rescue dog, guard-dog, tracking dog, assistant to the deaf, sheepdog, sniffer dog. Its intelligent, dependable and loyal nature allow the German shepherd to lay claim to its largest honour role — one of the most popular family dogs.

The popularity reflects the intelligence of this breed, which can be trained to accommodate multiple responsibilities while still maintaining its own individuality. The German shepherd has innate protective instincts and will be a natural protector of a family and their possessions. They should never be trained as a guard-dog at home, as they could exhibit aggressive characteristics at times when they are just not required.

Most owners agree that the temperament of the German shepherd is its single most important attribute; the breed should display steady nerves, self-assurance and be totally tractable. If you want a German shepherd, get to know both parents; if mum and dad aren't relaxed, self-confident, amiable individuals then look elsewhere for your puppy.

The breed enthusiasts have made great headway in decreasing the problem of hereditary diseases. Ensure you are given copies of certificates clearing both parents of hip and elbow dysplasia. If you need a hand understanding whether or not the certificates are good, talk to your local vet — they will decipher the scientific jargon and give you a comprehensible answer.

The short coat of a German shepherd is deceptive so you're best warned now that they should be given weekly brushing. The German shepherd has a thick double coat (topcoat and undercoat) which it generally sheds. While the change of seasons brings on the most shedding of hair, coat loss occurs all year round, so your vacuum-cleaning skills will be put to great use.

Every potential owner needs to be acutely aware that this breed requires socialisation, obedience training and reasonable exercise. These requirements fulfilled, they become a wonderful part of the family: loyal, loving, ready to protect your possessions and family with their own life.

Golden retriever

Golden retrievers act as if no one in the world would ever hurt them, and in turn they never deliberately hurt a soul. Their gentle caring manners are enhanced by their soft, teddy-bear-like appearance, and everyone *loves* a teddy bear. So trustworthy and trainable are they that the breed has often been utilised as guide-dogs for the blind.

Nature too, is pleased with the balanced shape of the breed, allowing them the longevity that they deserve, generally twelve to fourteen years. They do enjoy exercise and are particularly good swimmers, but they are not the type of dog that would protest with incessant barking should they miss a daily walk — they're just as happy sitting on the lounge, relaxing with the rest of the family.

They are gregarious, enjoying most their family's company. Golden retrievers will bark to alert you to the presence of a stranger but are not particularly known for their guard-dog abilities, though they can be protective of children in the family.

The luxurious, thick double coat affords good weather-resistance properties but the extra feathering does require some maintenance. A thorough, forceful brushing twice weekly, removing all knots and dead coat, will be enough to keep the dog clean so you can allow it to come inside. Alternatively, some owners elect to have the feathering clipped off every couple of months or so.

There have been four areas of heritable conditions of concern in the golden retriever. Eye problems have occurred with sufficient frequency to have ethical breeders ensure breeding animals are checked by a specialist veterinary ophthalmologist. Two orthopaedic (bone) problems that are screened for are hip dysplasia and elbow dysplasia; certificates clearing both parents should be sighted before buying a puppy. Congenital heart defects have also been seen in golden retrievers so a clearance by a veterinary cardiologist is a must prior to breeding.

Because it is such a gentle, loving dog, caring of very young children and attentive to its owner's requirements, the golden retriever has been classified by many knowledgeable dog people as the number one family dog.

Hungarian Vizsla

A sleek, elegant, all-purpose gun dog, the Vizsla is a popular family dog in its native home of Hungary. They are finicky about cleanliness, easy to toilet-train and adapt well to living in small homes. Their short, velvety coat is a striking, rich russet-gold colour. Zsa Zsa Gabor's love of this attractive breed increased their popularity in the USA.

The Vizsla is easily trained and responsive to gentle, correct handling. A reasonably lively dog that needs to stretch its limbs daily, the Vizsla is suited to an active family, especially if there's someone that enjoys jogging. Be aware, this is a retrieving dog that loves working in water so if you have a backyard pool, secure fencing is required unless you are prepared to have the dog in the water on hot days.

The Vizsla stands around 60 cm and weighs 24 to 30 kg. Hip dysplasia does plague the breed somewhat so only purchase a pup from parents that have a low hip score. Also, get your pup thoroughly checked upon purchase as the breed currently has a high rate of congenital heart murmurs.

Being active, intelligent, working gun dogs, they have a propensity to bark, alerting everyone to the presence of not only strangers but birds, lizards or any other creature that attracts their attention. Consequently, if you decide on a Vizsla, give it plenty of exercise and commit to five minutes of obedience training each day for their mental stimulation. Make sure you enrich their environment during the day with lots of toys, a maze (if you're up to building one) and even a radio (they prefer classical music — truly).

Their very short coat means no grooming and many people have found this breed suitable for allergy sufferers. Washing can be a ten-minute shampoo and rinse or a 30-second wipe-down with a damp cloth — they really are a very low-maintenance dog in the grooming department but remember their need for exercise and training.

Labrador retriever

This good Samaritan of the canine world can be found assisting humans in many areas of modern day life. The best-known role for this most dependable of dogs is as a guide-dog for the blind. They have also been used as bomb detection dogs. A keen working dog, the labrador is a sensible and sensitive dog that has consistently been popular as a family dog. So adaptable is this breed that with correct socialisation and training, they can receive a healthy workout from the most arduous of toddlers, be involved in doggie sports, or relax quietly in the company of older people.

The qualities of the labrador led to the animal becoming the most popular breed in the 1970s and this led to indiscriminate breeding and a deterioration of the breed. Australian breeders have worked hard to eradicate uncharacteristic behaviour, such as aggression, and have been rewarded by excellent animals. Australian-bred labradors are sought after by overseas breeders because of their soundness and temperament.

There is a concern that the breed is again increasing in popularity, and indiscriminate breeding has produced labradors with various problems. Prospective buyers should ask for copies of veterinary certificates, clearing the parents as much as possible from heritable defects. Most of all, a buyer should inspect the mother and father of a pup to ensure the temperament is exactly what should be expected from this most lovable of breeds. Never accept excuses about a labrador's character; they're not a protective breed but a gregarious family companion. They do have an extreme devotion to their family but they should be sufficiently confident and trusting to accept strangers approved by their owner.

One habit that the labrador is renowned for is scrounging food. They are great eaters yet will live on very little food. Never have your labrador overweight especially in the first twelve months of life as this might create bone and joint problems that could otherwise be avoided.

Develop a relationship with a labrador pup and it will last forever — you'll never forget that special dog with soft eyes, ever-wagging otter-like tail and warm heart.

Pekingese

So often I'm asked why I bother recommending the Pekingese to people as a pet. They have deformed faces, deformed legs, eye problems and are not the hardiest of dogs. The fact that they need so much care is exactly why I recommend them. Many people want, indeed need, a dog that is totally dependent upon them; often they openly admit that their Pekingese is a child substitute.

A Pekingese needs daily grooming and powdering to remove any unwanted material that might cling to their coat. They require the folds of skin on the face to be properly cleaned and dried. Their eyes should be washed with saline if any matter builds up on them and they may require daily eye drops or ointment to keep the eyes healthy.

Not uncommonly, the skin folds on the cheeks can rub against the eyeball itself, hence the need to keep this area clean, free from infection and tissue swelling. If it continues to be a problem then the skin folds should have the hair removed and a lubricating eye ointment applied directly to them. Professional advice may even suggest the folds need to be surgically reduced. The eyes of the Peke are probably its Achilles tendon, as another problem that can occur is prolapse of the eyeball (it literally pops out of the socket). It occurs if excess pressure builds up as a result of straining and quick veterinary attention must be sought if the eyeball is to be saved. See page 199 for more detail.

They are the ultimate lap dog, happiest when seated with their owner, interested in neither patrolling grounds nor gallivanting through gardens. Good natured and hardier than they make out, they are very affectionate and accepting of all the comforts you may wish to lavish on them.

Poodle

Poodles boost your ego like no other breed of dog, looking longingly at you, their owner, and almost ignoring anyone else. They are loyal and brave and come in any size to suit your home. There are toy poodles (the smallest stands at 28 cm), miniature poodles (standing to 38 cm) and standard poodles, the largest, are often well in excess of 60 cm.

The poodles' guarding ability should never be underestimated as even the tiny toy will bark at the approach of strangers. And don't be fooled by their somewhat delicate presentation. Much attention is given to their unique clip but they have effective, punishing jaws. The standard poodle has been used as a police dog in the past. And in the seventeenth century, Prince Rupert of the Rhine, known for his prowess on European battlefields, had a constant poodle companion named 'Boy', that reputedly saved his life.

While the coat of a poodle seems to be a great deal of work, it can be easily cut short every two to three months. The coat has the advantage of being very woolly and not shedding like most short-coated breeds, thus making the poodle an ideal dog for people who suffer allergies.

There are several health problems and these depend upon the size of poodle you select. Standard poodles suffer from hip dysplasia so parents need low hip scores. They can also get bloat so ensure you feed highly concentrated, easily digestible food and always in the cool of the day. Miniatures and toys suffer from eye defects, so breeding stock must be examined by a specialist veterinary ophthalmologist. Also, in the two smaller sizes, the kneecaps can congenitally dislocate so have a vet examine your pup before or shortly after purchase.

This gregarious, totally loyal, intelligent, elegant canine is an ideal family companion.

Pug

The cheekiest of all breeds of dog, the pug shows great adaptability. With origins that saw the ancestors of this breed shrouded in luxury with the royal families of ancient China, the pug now has followings in every walk of life. From you, the pug will seek a cuddle or a game and preferably both. And although ever faithful to its owner, the pug will seek those same comforts from a passing stranger, acting without fear or favour in its selection of a friend.

The most muscular of all the toy breeds, the pug is sturdy in build yet able to maintain itself with little exercise. Combine this with only minor needs in the grooming department, the pug adapts well as a companion and confidant for the elderly. Ask this snuffly-nosed character to mix with children and the pug will fulfil the task admirably. Given the mouth structure and soft lip folds, the pug couldn't deliver a punishing bite even if he wanted to. This is because of his short foreface.

The pug is fastidious in its presentation, enjoying a regular bath to ensure its own personal cleanliness. They are easily toilet-trained and readily accept going to the toilet in a confined area of the yard, but you will need to instil this practice early in their training.

The negative aspects of this breed stem from the accentuated shortening of the muzzle. The wrinkles around the face should be kept clean. They have a tendency to snort through the wrinkled up nose. Excess breathing noise and snoring may arise because of the convoluted soft tissue and often elongated soft palate which interferes with the clear exchange of air at the voice box (larynx). Finally, it is possible for an eyeball to pop out if the area is placed under excess pressure. See page

199 for more information. Being large, round and prominent, their eyes can easily be subjected to injury, so care is needed to avoid repeated harm, possibly leading to permanent damage.

During hot weather, particular attention is needed to avoid overheating, as poor respiration will mean difficult cooling. Lots of cool areas around the house, even ice blocks in their drinking water will assist in making life comfortable for this good natured character.

3. How do I know if I'm buying my pup from a good breeder?

Once you've selected a breed that suits your situation, find out what heritable defects occur within the breed. The best person to consult with is your local vet so it's worth making an appointment and asking about the breed. Some breeders will talk to you about the pros and cons of the breed so it is very worthwhile attending a couple of local dog shows to access at least four breeders. The honest breeder will not be afraid to disclose any problems with their breed of dog because they want their buyers to be well informed about potential problems.

The trap that nearly all novice buyers (and even many experienced purchasers) fall into is the belief that pedigree papers for a dog must guarantee quality. However, most pedigrees do little in assisting a purchaser as few have meaningful information on the soundness of ancestors. Information on animals that are screened for heritable diseases are only now being placed on pedigrees. Having information about each animal's health status on a pedigree gives more information to potential purchasers and allows breeders to assess their performance over generations for inherited diseases in their breeding lines.

When you meet the breeder you should ask about guarantees; ethical breeders have no trouble giving written guarantees for their stock. They can't guarantee that a pup won't develop problems, but they should offer to replace or refund if a pup you buy develops symptoms of a debilitating heritable disease during the first two years of life. It's unfair to expect a breeder to guarantee an animal for the whole of the dog's life or to expect a refund if the dog has a minor defect that does not affect the function of the pup.

Good breeders will invite you to make an appointment to check that you are a suitable person to own one of their puppies. A kennel doesn't necessarily mean a physical set up of many dog runs or some special canine-housing complex. Many people have just one breeding animal or just a few bitches at home but breed excellent quality dogs in their backyard. Don't be put off by someone honest enough to tell you this is their first attempt at breeding. Novice breeders are often more conscientious, ensuring that the mother has been tested for all possible diseases, taking nothing for granted and caring to make certain that she wants for nothing. Always check that the important basic requirements are provided as well as some added extras: hygiene, good nutrition, worming, vaccination and socialisation.

When you visit the litter, cleanliness is paramount. Not just the immediate area containing the puppies but wherever dogs are kept. This will give a clear indication of the care placed into breeding dogs. Lethargic, introverted or even unkempt, dirty pups are all a sign of a breeder that has not taken time to socialise the litter, let alone feed or worm the pups correctly. The pups should be full of energy, very keen for a game or at least some interaction with a visitor that shows interest in them.

Analyse this to see if a breeder is trustworthy:

1 Have you spoken to lots of breeders about the breed you want?
2 Is the breeder you selected prepared to talk to you about the breed?
3 Will they openly discuss problems that are generally known to exist within the breed?
4 Can they show you authentic evidence of screening tests that the parents have undergone?
5 If a DNA test is available for any heritable disease known in the breed, will they allow you to have the pup tested before you purchase?
6 Will the breeder help you contact people who have previously bought puppies from them?

7 Is the breeder prepared to show you the written guarantee/contract that you will both sign when purchasing a pup?

8 Is the care of the dogs shown by the breeder reasonable, and the general environment of the dogs clean and not overcrowded?

9 Will the breeder allow you to leave a blanket for your pup that you can take home later?

10 Will you receive a copy of the diet chart, worming program and vaccination schedule when you buy your pup?

Seven is the lucky number; a no to this question and it's time to find another breeder for your future pup. If there is contract or guarantee, make sure that it is fair and equitable without placing unreasonable requirements on either side. You might even want to have a solicitor check the contract before signing.

No to more than four of these would mean you need to seriously consider finding another breeder.

4. What do I look out for if I don't get my puppy from a breeder?

If you don't get your puppy from a breeder, you can acquire one from a welfare centre such as the Animal Welfare League, from a Lost Dogs' Home or the RSPCA, or a council dog pound. You can also purchase a pup from a pet shop, or you might be given one from someone who has a litter of pups that they can't keep.

Of course, getting a dog from a lost dog's home or the local pound is a great thing because you are giving a dog a second chance. When you consider the thousands of unwanted dogs that are killed every year, rescuing just one life is important.

Institutions that take care of lost and unwanted dogs usually have the dog de-sexed and vaccinated before it leaves, so you can trust that a full veterinary inspection has been performed. Most of these organisations have someone trained in canine behaviour and the dogs are assessed to ascertain if they are suitable for a new home. The dogs will have been well-handled so any that have severely anti-social temperaments would usually be eliminated from a re-housing program. Dog pounds are also addressing these issues by ensuring their staff are trained to develop systems for successful re-homing of dogs that have been found or surrendered. Some pounds are so successful that a few local councils have developed 'no kill' policy for the dogs that come under their jurisdiction. Of course, dangerous or extremely sick dogs would be euthanised, but all other dogs are kept until the right home comes along. This has been made possible through positive identification and education of the general public to develop responsible dog ownership.

Even though the institutions are doing a great job of re-housing dogs, no system is perfect. Firstly, make sure that you can return the dog over the next few weeks if things don't turn out as you expected. And having decided to take a dog from a shelter or dog pound, you need to be prepared to spend some hours with your selection. Walk around with the dog to see if you relate well to each other, making sure the animal is well socialised, accepting other humans that are around it and not charging out to attack other dogs or people.

Some problems won't surface until you get the dog home. For example, the dog you've chosen may have been an escape artist in the past, so if it exits your property despite good fencing, you may end up paying a council fine. Alternatively, your beautiful landscaping could well be destroyed, and you might discover that this is the very reason your dog was in the pound. Once the dog settles in, it could become a nuisance barker - this must definitely be cured if you don't want your surrounding neighbourhood to exorcise you from your premises. You need to discuss these things with the people you are acquiring the dog from. They may not have a full history but should do their best to assist as these are caring people that only want the dog to go to a good and responsible home.

Buying from a pet shop is different again. Most pet shops fail to give any reasonable guarantee other than general medical health for the first week or so. They will rarely guarantee against heritable defects (see page 19) so it becomes a case of 'buyer beware'. However, if you buy a pup from a pet shop, the dog should have at least current vaccination certificate and a recent health clearance by a registered vet. If symptoms such as not eating, vomiting or diarrhoea develop in the first two weeks, report it immediately to your vet and the pet shop proprietor. Most shop owners will be genuinely concerned. The same health rules - no potbelly, clear eyes, pink gums apply to these pups as to pups you buy from a breeder (see page 26).

5. How do I pick the right puppy from a litter?

When selecting a pup for your home you need to think about which breed's characteristics best suit you and which individual pup in a selected litter will cope with living with you and your family.

In selecting a pup from a litter, you need to seriously consider your own personality and you should be honest with yourself about the type of dog you want. Sometimes, you will have no choice as to which pup you can purchase from a litter but you still need to make a decision. Is the pup that is offered for sale to you the type of animal you want to live with for the next twelve or so years? You may forfeit a deposit, but you need to be satisfied that the pup is the right dog for you and your family.

The pup that rushes out to meet all visitors may be more social, but its exuberance may be more than you can live with. As long as the litter is social then the pup that takes its time, is more laid back with an overall calmer approach to everything, is most likely to be the more successful family member.

If the whole litter is shy and retiring then you should probably shift your purchase to another breeder. There are some critical periods of development of a pup's temperament, many of which occur in the first six weeks of life. If the correct nurturing of their personality or temperament does not occur, permanent behavioural problems may be created.

The fine line that you have to draw is the difference between a shy pup and one that is calm and quieter. The quieter pup does not resent being patted or picked up; it accepts any overtures from you, placidly and without resentment. The shy pup not only resents being cuddled and patted but may even retaliate. If you look at a pup's eyes as you approach it for a cuddle, you will immediately know if there is any sign of fear in the animal. And remember, a dog that is fearful is the most dangerous, especially if it feels cornered.

Analyse this to pick the right puppy:

1   Is the litter sufficiently social to give you confidence that the pup has been properly reared?

2   Will the pup you've chosen happily allow you to pick it up then cuddle it into your arms?

3   Does the pup I've chosen enjoy a simple game with me such as chasing my hand or even retrieving a toy?

4   Is the pup attentive of its environment, looking quietly but confidently at new visitors?

5   Are the puppies happy to be out in the open rather than hiding in corners or under furniture?

6   When disturbed unexpectedly, do the puppies casually look up from their bed or resting place instead of immediately becoming vocal, barking while running backwards into a corner?

No to four or more means it's time to look at another litter.

No to question 2 means you need to closely examine if this is the pup for you.

6. How do I know if I've got a healthy pup?

There are three points you have to consider when assessing a pup's health. Check that the puppy

- is free of any infectious or parasitic disease
- has been cleared as much as possible for heritable defects
- has a healthy mind.

For your dog to have a healthy body, it should have been properly fed, wormed and vaccinated. The breeder should talk to you about the pup's feeding and worming program and provide you with a vaccination certificate. A reasonable worming schedule would see the pup wormed at two, four and six weeks of age then you should be advised to dose the pup within 48 hours of purchase and again at twelve weeks of age. While few breeders recommend worming so soon after you acquire your pup, it gives you the assurance that the pup is free of intestinal adult worms. Also, it helps keep your yard clean of worm eggs from infected faecal material.

A pup that has been wormed and fed correctly will be round and full looking, have a shiny coat, plenty of energy, bright eyes that are free of discharge, rich pink coloured gums and a distinctive, pleasant puppy breath.

By contrast, pups that have worms will have a dull coat, a potbelly, loose motions, pale gums from anaemia and, commonly, bad breath. They may also be lethargic or tire quickly. Unhealthy pups will often have a discharge from the eyes, smelly ears because of excess wax or possibly infection, and sometimes splayed feet reflecting a poorly balanced diet. Look closely at the pup's skin, especially on the belly and on the base of the tail to examine the area for fleas. Dirty pups that have parasites on the outside will most likely have worms on the inside. Cleanliness may not be next to godliness but it's certainly paramount to good health.

Some diseases, such as hip or elbow dysplasia, cannot be assessed at birth and you have to rely on genetic information. Begin by checking on the parents; you should sight certificates for both the mother and father of the litter. Secondly, though this might be more difficult, find out if either parent has had previous puppies — any problems may have shown up in these litters. For example, if many offspring from a sire or dam suffer from allergic skin diseases, this may be your cue to look elsewhere for the pup of your dreams, otherwise you may become a frequent visitor to your vet.

An excellent idea is to take the pup to your local vet in the first few days after purchase. A thorough physical examination by a professional can help eliminate any doubt about the health of your pup. Plus, it gives you the opportunity to establish a relationship with your vet. Don't forget to ask about availability of after-hours emergency service by the practice you choose.

Any genuine breeder should guarantee the pup's physical health from infectious diseases for at least one to two weeks in case it is incubating something at the time of purchase. It is not a crime for a breeder to sell a pup that is incubating a disease or harbouring the potential to develop a heritable defect. In fact, most breeders feel terrible if this ever happens because, apart from anything else, it reflects badly on their reputation. If your pup develops signs of any problems then talk to the breeder as soon as possible. The reasonable ones will be concerned and endeavour to assist in any way possible.

Analyse this to see if you have a healthy pup:

1   Is your pup typical of an exuberant, active youngster?
2   Are the clear eyes, shiny coat, healthy-coloured pink gums and shiny coat obvious?
3   Regardless of examinations, is the breeder willing to give written guarantees about your pup's health?
4   Are you given clear instructions about the puppy's past and future worming program?
5   Is a vaccination certificate is supplied with the pup, signed by a registered vet with the date the pup was vaccinated and indicating when the next booster is due?
6   Does the pup have a healthy appetite, readily eating its food?
7   Have you checked that your puppy's poo is well-formed and not loose or sloppy?

More than anything else, recognise the characteristics in question 2. Without those signs, a pup cannot be considered healthy and you should choose another one.

7. What vaccinations does my puppy require?

There are six main vaccinations that your puppy should receive:
- canine parvovirus
- distemper
- hepatitis
- canine parainfluenza virus
- *Bordetella bronchisepta*
- leptospirosis

The problem with vaccinations is that you do not see the benefits. You can't actually see your dog fighting off a lethal disease because it has been vaccinated. Remember that the diseases that vaccines protect against are still out there. It's easy to become complacent when you don't actually see the pitfalls of not vaccinating. If a few pups miss out on vaccinations, chances are that they may even get through life without an incident, but this is hardly proof that vaccinations aren't necessary. When many pups in a population do not receive vaccinations then the diseases that are endemic in our society will strike hard, fast and without favour or mercy.

Vaccinations themselves can cause problems. A few dogs will be adversely affected each year, so while certain individuals may react badly to vaccinations, the overall the benefits outweigh the risks. Without vaccines, hundreds of animals and thousands of humans would suffer.

Canine parvovirus, distemper and hepatitis are three potentially lethal diseases for dogs found throughout the world. Parvovirus commenced in canines during the late 1970s, presenting as a severe gastroenteritis. It strips the internal lining of the gut causing the infected dog to dehydrate and even haemorrhage. Puppies are at greatest risk, with thousands of deaths being attributable to parvovirus right through the 1980s. The virus is still a threat in the dog world and will strike down any susceptible subject.

Distemper is a virus that hits quickly when contact is made with an unprotected victim. Dogs will present with a fever, signs of pneumonia and usually develop severe neurological signs such as seizures. Death is not always the conclusion, but animals that do recover are usually left with permanent defects.

Canine hepatitis is a virus that affects the liver. The function of this organ is drastically impaired so massive supportive therapy is imperative in dogs infected with the virus. Many dogs have died as a result of this condition.

Vaccines for these diseases are essential and commence at around six weeks of age. Be aware that maternal antibodies can interfere greatly with vaccination at this time and check with the breeder or vet that all is fine. All pups need boosters at twelve weeks and, depending upon the type of vaccination, some also require a third booster at sixteen weeks of age. You must keep your pup well away from areas where there are other dogs until fourteen days after its last vaccination. From then on, annual vaccinations are recommended to maintain your dog's protection against these deadly viruses.

Kennel cough is a highly infectious disease related to the influenza virus that causes a persistent, hacking cough. The two bugs that cause this cough are canine parainfluenza virus and *Bordetella bronchisepta*. The latter organism can be transferred to children, so care needs to be taken to ensure no cross-infection occurs. Vaccines for these two bugs are available and while they are effective, don't expect 100 per cent protection — like a flu vaccine for humans. Nevertheless, vaccinated animals that do contract the disease overcome it quickly if their immune system is otherwise healthy. Information on kennel cough is given on page 154.

Leptospirosis is a bacterium that can be carried by rodents. If a rat or mouse infected with leptospirosis urinates in a dog's drinking water (one of the most common methods of infecting dogs) or is caught and eaten by a dog (a frequent habit of terriers), the dog will be infected. Every few years outbreaks do occur, especially in city regions. The bacteria colonise in the kidneys;, resulting in jaundice and death due to renal failure. The whole problem can be avoided by annual vaccination for these bacteria.

Fortunately, the rabies virus is not found in every country throughout the world. Australia, New Zealand, and many other island countries are considered rabies-free, so rabies vaccination is not necessary. Where the virus is present in wild animals (for example, in foxes in France and in raccoons in the USA, dogs must be vaccinated annually. The virus is deadly and crosses the species barrier with ease. It attacks every tissue of the body, with affected animals developing a fear of water and eventually dying in terrible pain.

Herbal vaccines can give people a false sense of security. Dogs have some degree of natural immunity so sterile water and herbal vaccines work 50 per cent of the time.

Analyse this to work out what vaccinations your puppy requires:

1 Did you receive a vaccination certificate, signed by a registered vet, when you purchased a new puppy or adult dog?
2 Have you followed all the booster recommendations for your dog?
3 Does your dog need an extra vaccination booster two weeks before going to a boarding kennel?
4 Do you receive annual vaccination reminders for your pet?
5 Have you discussed with your vet what vaccines your dog needs?

8. How can I avoid first-night blues for my puppy?

The majority of novice dog owners will either tough out the first few nights, letting the pup cry, or they will relent, spoiling the pup by placing it in bed with them. Either way, the pup is suffering unduly. In the first instance, it will suffer because it's lonely, probably frightened and definitely sad. In the second instance, it will suffer because being in bed with its owner may or may not be comfortable, but sooner or later, the owner will need to leave the pup alone at night and this makes for a worse situation. Also, having a pup in bed with you may lead to the pup developing problems such as dominance behaviour.

Preparing for a new pup's first night must start well before you are scheduled to pick up your puppy. There are a number of things you can do to help the puppy settle into its new home.

Most breeders will allow you to leave a blanket with your pup (and the rest of the litter) for a couple of days. Prior to giving this blanket to the breeder, keep it on your bed for a day or so then place it in the box, laundry, kennel or wherever you intend the pup to sleep, for a few more days. Also, buy an indestructible toy which can be left with the litter. The blanket and the toy will go a long way into comforting the pup through the night. These objects will have the smell of the area the pup was born in, as well as its littermates and possibly also the mother. Surrounding the pup with familiar smells will mean more to your dog than anything else you can do.

Plan that first day properly to suit your puppy. Pick your pup up early, take it home and play with the little critter. This will assist the important bonding process and give your pup something else to think about rather than missing its mother and siblings.

When the pup seems tired, allow it to rest in the sleeping area you have selected. It's also a good idea to feed the pup in this area and leave it there with the food for a short period so it gets the idea that you will return. Do not go to the pup while it is crying — you're training the pup, not the pup training you. Frequent short periods of leaving the pup on its own during the day can assist in allowing it to accommodate the notion of being alone.

A radio placed on low volume will have the pup think there are people around, making the acceptance of solitude and confinement that much easier. The sleeping quarters you select for your pup should be dimly lit, warm, free of draughts, contain dry bedding and not allow access to things that can be destroyed. The toy that the pup brought home should be provided at this time, as should the blanket that had been previously left to gather smells from the breeder's property.

Hot water bottles can be helpful but not for rambunctious pups that may puncture the thing with their sharp milk teeth. An old ticking clock should not be discounted as it does mimic the heartbeat of littermates or at least provides a regular, rhythmic noise to distract the pup and help it sleep.

Analyse this to prepare for your puppy's homecoming:

1. Did you remember to give the breeder a blanket or solid toy to leave with the litter for a day or so?
2. Have you planned the pick-up day so as to minimise other commitments, allowing you most of the day to settle the pup into your home?
3. Is there an area set aside to provide a warm, secure and quiet place for the pup to sleep?
4. Have you bought an old clock or a toy that has a sound similar to a littermate's heartbeat?
5. Did you visit your new pup a few times before purchase?

As you analyse these questions, remember that you are trying to understand things from the dog's perspective, so 'think dog'.

9. What is hip dysplasia and how can I avoid it when buying a puppy?

To fully understand the term 'hip dysplasia' you need to know a little about the anatomy of the hip joint. Commonly classified as a ball-and-socket joint, it is a long bone that forms a ball shape at the end which fits into a deep socket. The ball is the upper section of the largest bone in the leg, the femur. The socket is a cave-like structure or indentation in the pelvis. For a ball-and-socket to work correctly the ball needs to be smooth, fitting securely into the socket. If the ball fits loosely in the socket, then as movement occurs the ball clunks or bashes in and out of the socket. This continually crashes the two surfaces together instead of a smooth roll of the ball through the arc of the socket. The crashing and bashing of the two surfaces causes roughening and abnormal wear of the bones that eventually results in total breakdown in the function of the ball-and-socket.

There are several reason why this simple ball-and-socket, namely the hip joint, can malfunction. The most common reason occurs when the ball section (the femoral head) does not sit tightly in the socket (the acetabulum) but rather sits out a little, resulting in a loose, sloppy joint. If the femoral head or ball pops right out of the socket, this is a dislocation and is referred to as luxation. When the ball is loose, sitting only slightly out of the socket but not dislocated, it is referred to as subluxation. If the joint is forced into bearing too much weight, the ball can push out slightly resulting in hip dysplasia. Don't let your dog become too fat as this can induce hip dysplasia.

The majority of hip dysplasia is not environmentally induced but is a hereditary condition. However, you can still purchase a pup and be reasonably confident that it will not grow to develop hip dysplasia.

While it is imperative that you seek a pup from parents that have been cleared for hip dysplasia, it is even better to buy from parents that already have offspring that have been cleared.

Once you purchase a pup, you need to ensure you provide the best environment that avoids stress to the hip joint. The most important issue is that of weight: never allow your pup to become fat. Err on the side of caution, keeping your pup leaner rather than slightly overweight. Next, don't overexercise young pups. Give them room to bound around and stretch their limbs, but avoid forcing mile after mile of jogging in the first nine months of their life. Similarly, avoid excess jumping, jarring or any exercise that places too much pressure on the hips. Dogs do the majority of weight bearing through the front legs (easily 70 per cent or more) so requiring them to continually climb stairs or in any way throw their weight to their hindquarters, further predisposes them to hip dysplasia.

While it all sounds terrible, most dogs do not develop debilitating hip dysplasia and with just a little effort and careful planning the problem can be avoided.

10. Do all dogs need training?

Since the origin of the species, dogs have been a pack animal, meaning that they have a definitive hierarchy with clear, exact rules. Dogs in a domestic household are no different, forming a pack with the family in which they live, be it one or more persons. The environment you provide will be critical in the dog's attainment of personality and position in the pack. Spoil your dog, never say no, forget to instil tolerance and patience, and you can promote the meekest animal into becoming a dominant, aggressive creature. With simple, clear rules set down by you, their pack leader, your dog will find order and fulfilment.

Temperament is determined by a combination of heritable factors and environmental circumstances. One of the aims of training is to provide an environment that nurtures positive reinforcement using gentle but persuasive methods of conditioning the dog towards desirable behaviours.

If you ever meet a well-mannered, properly trained dog, the first thing you notice is their calm, confident demeanour. Often, their primary concern is to focus on their owner/trainer but that doesn't mean they have a one-track mind about training or that they're not capable of individual thought or action. It simply reflects the bond that has developed between human and canine.

A well-trained dog is far less likely to bite and would never do so without a logical reason. The decision to bite would usually indicate that the person bitten has threatened the dog's master or property. Trained dogs usually will not bite when threatened but will rather wait until they are injured. A trained dog quickly assesses the danger so if teased by a child, it will find refuge in distancing itself from the menace in preference to launching into an attack. This, more than any other reason, is why every dog should have some training.

Dogs that are trained are handled more frequently. This touch assists in bond development and makes the dog easier to handle should it ever get sick or injured. This may not seem important at the start, but such tolerance could save your dog's life. Just imagine how much simpler it is to give a dog a tablet or place a bandage over a bleeding wound when the animal is used to being handled.

Having learnt the basic rules of patience, tolerance and confidence, a trained dog is less likely to bark without reasonable cause. The most notable reason for dogs to enter into nuisance barking is sheer boredom, which is greatly relieved by regular obedience training.

Whenever I hear people complain about a particular aspect of their dog's behaviour, the first question I ask is, 'Has the dog ever had any formal obedience lessons?' The answer is nearly always yes until the owner is asked to elaborate; then you learn that, at best, the lessons amounted to puppy school when the dog was a few months old. Training needs to continue throughout your dog's life; even five minutes a day reinforces formal training. If a trained dog lapses into some undesirable behaviour, the owner can usually quickly change it. Untrained dogs have more difficulty accepting change.

Problems such as biting, barking and digging have become more severe with increased dog ownership in our society. The cause of these problems lies not with the canine but the owners who fail to understand the dog's needs. Choose the breed carefully, as some breeds have less need for their owner's full commitment.

A dominant breed must be formally trained, and there are no

short cuts. A client of mine found it difficult to find the time to take his Rottweiler to obedience school. Instead, he thought he would train the animal at home. Each time I saw his dog it growled in an aggressive manner. One day, unsurprisingly, it bit its owner severely. That dog was euthanised, but he bought another Rottweiler and it is now listed as a difficult, potentially aggressive dog at my clinic. Dominant dogs should be trained and at an obedience school that believes in firm discipline with praise for correct, gentle behaviour.

Put simply, a trained dog becomes a special friend, able to share many experiences with you and your family.

Analyse this to see if your dog needs training:

1   Would you prefer to have your dog inside from time to time?
2   When visitors arrive, would you prefer not to race around, locking the dog away before it bites someone?
3   Given a leash-free area for your dog, would you like to feel confident that it would come immediately when you call?
4   Do you want a dog that you can leave alone at home, confident it won't develop bad habits, such as barking and digging?
5   Would you like to know that your dog will protect you if needed?

Yes to any of the questions means you must consider some time for your dog's obedience lessons.

11. When should a dog commence training?

Training patterns can commence as soon as your new puppy or dog arrives home. Think about:

- where you want the dog to go to the toilet
- the area you have selected for sleeping
- what you prefer the dog to chew rather than your slippers
- where and when the dog will eat
- instilling good eating habits.

All these issues and more are taught by dog owners the world over without the need for formal lessons. In fact, owners usually do not even realise they are teaching their dogs.

No matter how old your dog is, not withstanding the obvious physical limitations of a geriatric, it can be trained. Indeed, acquiring an older dog can be a rewarding experience for you but often, in the initial stages, the experience can be traumatic for the dog. Proper, gentle training methods assist greatly in the settling-in period for the dog so that the new family member quickly learns the housekeeping rules and can live happily in the household. This means any unacceptable social behaviours that have already become part of the dog's habitual actions should quickly disappear.

Behaviour is determined by an interaction between what is inherited and what is learnt. Older dogs can be trained but there are periods in a dog's life where learning is accelerated. In the first six weeks of a dog's life, several milestones of personality and behaviour are reached. It is necessary to ensure you buy from a good breeder who takes time to socialise and sensitise the pups before you purchase your animal.

Children can form a critical part of a dog's socialisation and it is important that they interact as early as possible. Some breeders will overprotect their pups, becoming concerned that children may hurt them or that by taking the pups out, they may be exposed to disease. The worst disease any dog can get is that of a fearful mind. Don't let anyone tell you differently — socialise your pup as soon as you get it.

Sensitive periods for dogs must be considered especially in the first twelve months of life. Puppyhood can hold lots of adventures but if a dog is severely frightened or continually admonished then this could break the dog, even turning the animal into a 'fear biter' to protect itself.

During these important stages of puppyhood and adolescence, a dog's training needs to be positive in its construction, with lots of praise when the dog is gently persuaded to perform in the correct, socially acceptable manner. How you stage the lessons is up to you. Every experience in a dog's life is a learning exercise — do it wisely and your dog can start learning from the moment it enters the household.

Analyse this to see when to start training your dog:

1   Do I want my dog to know it has a special place to sleep, a place it can go if it's being harassed by children?
2   Do I want my dog to confine its toilet habits to one area of the yard?
3   Do I want my dog to know when it's feed time, to accept taking titbits, but never to snatch food?
4   Do I want my dog to be a sociable member of my family?

Yes to any of these questions means that training should commence immediately.

12. What is the best way to get my dog trained?

Dog training is a two-part process. The owner as well as the dog needs training, so the best person to train your dog is you. And the best place to train your dog is from home — not literally on the home property, but organise your dog's training from your home. Lessons can be accessed at any obedience school through either professional or weekly club sessions. The critical thing to do is to train at home in between formal weekly lessons. Some dog owners mistakenly believe that the dog needs hours of laborious training, when only ten minutes a day, four times a week is enough.

Every dog will vary with the amount of training they require, but the golden rule is not to bore your dog to death. Over-trained dogs become more like machines than dogs, losing their own identity and even some degree of dignity. Dogs that are never trained fail to develop certain abilities to reason. But placed into the right environment, trained dogs quickly develop a sense of self-worth and responsibility. They become a valuable family member.

The other training option is to use a professional trainer, but I don't recommend this for several reasons.

Firstly, a good professional handler can easily train most dogs to respond to simple commands such as sit, stand, stay, drop, heel and come. They can even teach the dog more complicated tasks like retrieving over an obstacle or tracking a person through the bush. But once the dog returns home from training camp, the lessons are usually not properly reinforced because the owner needs far more time at training camp than the dog.

Secondly, the owner has not developed a good working relationship with the dog and probably does not know how to reinforce the training. They may love the dog, and desire to have a dog that is well-behaved, but with dogs you only get out what you put in.

If you decide to use a professional trainer ensure it is not a quick-fix course of less than six weeks. A good professional trainer will take time, using gentle but persuasive methods to condition your dog to correctly respond to verbal commands. Once the dog is confident in the level of the response required, the handler will ask you to return with the animal for several lessons so that you can be trained to continue the conditioning program at home. During these sessions, you will be able to raise problems that occur with your dog at home so the trainer understands your particular needs.

It takes time and patience to learn to understand why dogs do the things they do and the dog learns your expectations. During training you will hopefully learn to 'think dog' and if you're enjoying yourself enough, you might decide to go on to even bigger and better things in dog training. Somewhere out there, the next doggie star is in the making and it might even be your dog.

Analyse this to see where your dog should be trained:
1 Do you want the dog to reliably respond to your commands?
2 Can you spend ten minutes per day, four days each week plus a concentrated two-hour lesson with an instructor once per week for six to eight weeks?
3 Have you established a warm and affectionate relationship with your dog?
4 Does your dog fear you?

If you answer yes to the first three questions, the best place to train your dog is at home, and you should take yourself and your dog to a weekly lesson by an instructor. Practise for ten minutes per day at home and in six weeks you will have achieved many goals — not necessarily all the unrealistic achievements you expected, but you'll definitely have a well-behaved family dog.

13. How do I teach my dog to come when called?

If you have been chasing your dog you have probably unwittingly taught him a new game called 'catch me if you can'. By chasing him all over the paddock, your dog has learnt that once he is off the lead, you are prepared to spend a great deal of time trying to catch him. Your dog is quite happy to play chasey and since you are the pack leader, the dog gets to play with the number one love of his life, and receives the attention he thinks he deserves.

You can train him to come, and a good time to start is at meal-time. On the assumption that you do not feed your dog ad lib or always have food out for your dog, mealtime should result in the dog wanting to come to you. With the meal prepared, call your dog using his name and immediately saying the word 'come'. If the dog is so interested in his food that he is standing right next to you, simply take one step away from him and call as described. The point of the exercise is to have your dog rewarded by a meal on arriving when he is called. The distance the dog needs to travel when he gets there is not significant – what matters is that he did come when called.

If your dog enjoys particularly tasty little morsels of food (small pieces of barbecued chicken are excellent) then utilise these through-out the day by calling your dog's name, telling him to come and rewarding with positive reinforcement via a small piece of chicken. While the dog is eating, don't forget to continually praise him by saying 'good dog'. This develops a Pavlovian response with the dog associating the term 'good dog' with the pleasant sensation of eating something he likes. If he is distracted by something that captures his interest more than your calling or a piece of chicken, stop calling him. By continually calling him when he is ignoring you, you bring undone much of your work up to that point.

Invest in a lead made of either webbing or leather, between two and four metres long. It's now time to take the dog out for walks where you allow the dog to venture to the full length of the lead then call him back. Remember to use just his name and the command 'come' and when the dog responds by returning to you, give him lots of praise. It's also a great idea to have with you some of those tasty morsels that began to help the dog to focus. If the dog doesn't respond by returning to you, utilise the lead to ensure the desired behaviour. At the end of the exercise when the dog is right next to you, praise and a little bit of food will go a long way to ensuring that soon you won't need to use the lead as often.

This on-lead exercise needs to be performed in the park where the dog has learnt to run away from you. How long this whole proce-dure takes depends on the number of times you perform the exercise throughout any one week and the consistency you display when he correctly responds to the recall. Performed correctly, consistently reinforced and patiently rewarded, the dog can be taught to come when called in less than three weeks.

If you are still not confident that your dog will readily return to you, you may wish to invest in an even longer lead. Take your dog out for a walk with both leads on him. At the park make a show of taking off the shorter lead by throwing it a few feet away so that the dog sees the lead on the ground. Allow him to wander off to the full length of the longer lead and try your luck at calling him back to you. If the response is good then it is time to try the big test.

On the day of the big test, when you have given your dog a free run off-lead and something in his memory reminds him of running away and what fun it was remaining just out of your reach, don't despair quite yet. You still have one trick left up your sleeve. Rather than chasing your dog and re-establishing the old pattern of play, run away from him, calling his name to attract him. Your unusual behaviour, plus a twang of separation anxiety combined with years of evolution that instruct every dog to follow the pack leader, will usually result in your dog trying to run you down.

Once you capture your charge, do not under any circumstances admonish him as this will make it more difficult next time. The absolute key to training a dog to come when called is never to chastise your dog when he comes to you. If you structure the dog's environment correctly and understand that while firmness is important, consistency, direction and praise are by far the quickest teachers, you will find that reprimand of any kind is rarely required to correctly train a dog.

14. Can a dog be taught to stay when told?

All dogs can be taught to sit or lie down and stay in that position, but be aware that some breeds do not lend themselves to such obedience training. The degree of confidence you have in your dog staying in the same position will depend on the amount of training you give the dog in this exercise.

A good starting point when teaching the stay exercise is to place the dog's evening meal on the floor, then sit your dog in front of the food and hold him there while telling him to 'stay'. Hold the dog there for ten seconds then release him by saying 'good boy' and allowing him access to the food. This continues daily until the dog will automatically sit in front of his dinner and wait to be released by your command. The period that he is asked to stay in the sit position lengthens until you are confident that your dog can sit there for one minute before you release him to the pleasures of his gastronomic interests.

After the first week of this teaching, your dog should be placed on a lead during a daily training period, then made to sit on command and told to stay. It is usual practice for the dog to be sitting on the handler's left-hand side at this point. The handler, having told the dog to stay, takes one step with the right foot and stands immediately in front of the dog. Should the dog go to break (that is, move) the handler should quickly sit the dog back down using the command 'sit', and then say 'stay', ensuring the dog hasn't moved very far away from his original position.

Wait there for thirty seconds or so, then to ensure the dog doesn't anticipate when it's time to release him from the stay position, walk to the left of the dog then around behind him and eventually back to where you initially told him to stay. After five to ten seconds there, bend down and praise your dog for not moving.

Your dog will have learnt many points in this exercise. In the first instance, he has obviously learnt the stay word. Secondly, he has learnt to feel safe while you are out of sight, albeit for a fleeting moment while you are behind him. Thirdly, he has learnt that you will always return, making him feel secure in remaining in the position that he was told to stay. All this is reinforced by the praise you give him at the end of the exercise.

Repetition is the next big training tool, so this exercise should continue in this fashion for at least two weeks on a daily basis. After a fortnight of this exercise, the average dog will have learnt to stay without moving, at least while you are so close. The next step involves taking two steps away, then turning and facing the animal, remaining there for sixty seconds before returning to him in the same manner that you have been using previously. If he breaks without your consent, return to him immediately, chastising him with the word 'No!', and making him sit in the original position, telling him to stay while you again walk two paces back away. Praise must happen when you finally return to your dog, who can only get the message through your consistent and repetitive actions.

This continues for a fortnight, after which time you move further from the dog, while always having control of the exercise by leaving him on the lead. By now you should be able to walk to the end of a two to three metre lead, turn around and face him and leave him for a minute or three. Never leave your dog in the stay position for exactly the same time, as he learns to anticipate this time and becomes anxious if you do not return after the allotted period. Rather, randomise the time anywhere between thirty seconds to three minutes. Once your dog develops the confidence that you will return, and you are confident that he will stay, the next stage of the training can begin.

During this time, continue the stay exercise prior to feeding the dog. Again, use a varied stay period before releasing the dog to the meal.

The dog should be placed in the sit-stay position while you perform various tasks around the house. Washing the car, making the bed, doing some gardening, cooking the evening meal, reading a book or even watching television are all good opportunities to continue stabilising your dog to the stay exercise. With your dog in the formal sit position on your left hand side, tell him to stay, leave on your right foot as you have been doing for the last few weeks, then commence whatever task you have chosen. Your attention must be focused on the dog, not by staring directly at him, but rather watching him carefully through the corner of your eye, ensuring he does not move from where you have left him. While appearing to be uninterested in the dog's behaviour, if the dog breaks, quickly chastise him using the word no and return to him immediately, making him sit in the position. Again, leave your dog telling him to 'stay'. Return immediately to complete the task you were performing, always focusing on the dog without being obvious.

At first you shouldn't expect too much from your dog. Don't leave him in such a position for more than five minutes. As you build confidence in your dog's ability to behave the way you want, increase this time. During these types of exercises, the dog should always be in a comfortable place. Remember, if you are washing your car for example, cement or pavers become extremely warm in the sun, so do not ask your dog to sit on them for any length of time.

With patience, consistency and kindness your dog can be taught to stay in these circumstances for as long as is necessary. The next step is to teach him to stay while you go out of sight.

With your dog in a comfortable position in the yard, ask him to sit, tell him to stay and then go inside, keeping a constant watch through a window or around a corner of a door. Leave the dog for about three minutes then return to him, remembering to lavish him with praise once the exercise has been completed. Walk around your dog as you have always done, teaching him that the release comes when you ask him and that praise will always follow. The exercise continues in the backyard and the time lengthens and varies on a daily basis. Once you are confident that you can leave your dog, go inside and have a cup of coffee. Return to your dog, who is, hopefully, still in the same position. Now it is time for the next big test.

Find a park where dogs are allowed to be leash-free and which also has a building on it. If you drive to the park, do not leave your car near the building but rather far enough away that you need to walk at least some distance away from the car to get closer to the building. Tell your dog to sit and stay and walk towards the building, but don't go out of sight — rather turn around and stand watching your dog. After five minutes return to him, lavishing praise. This needs only to be repeated on a few occasions during a fortnightly period.

Once your dog realises that you will return to him even when left in a strange place, you can tell the dog to sit and stay and walk around behind the building, first keeping an eye on the dog by peeking around the corner. If all is going to plan, you will eventually be able to take a thermos with you and stop for that cup of coffee while you are waiting for time to pass before returning to your dog. The final big test comes when you park the car near the building and your dog has every confidence in you that you will return. Never get into your car and leave him unattended. Just simply hide behind the building for varying periods of time and always return to your dog, leaving him secure in the fact you will never abandon him.

The final phase of training requires distractions to be placed before the dog while he is in the sit-stay position and you are out of sight. Someone calling the dog, throwing a ball near him or running in front of him are all good distractions that a well-trained dog learns to ignore. The exercise requires the dog to be focused on you and you alone. This can only happen through a relationship of trust and love that takes time and effort.

15. Will my dog ever learn to lie quietly inside?

If you never taught children manners then no matter what age, if they came into a room with a plate full of biscuits on the coffee table, they would simply demolish all of them. The same principle applies to dogs. While certain aspects of your dog's behaviour are most definitely inherited, many of the behaviours that make dogs socially acceptable to humans need to be learnt.

Owners who find their dogs a nuisance whenever they are inside the house will tend to confine them to the backyard. This immediately takes away many of the advantages of owning a dog. Companionship, for example, is then confined only to those times when you are outside, but many enjoyable moments can be shared while you are sitting quietly with your dog by your side, simply stroking his head. For those dogs who also afford us the added security of protection, leaving them outside all the time most certainly decreases their effectiveness. Police report that many robberies have been prevented by a dog living happily inside. Nevertheless, should your dog not understand the manners required for living inside your house, his presence becomes difficult to tolerate and it is far easier to send him out the back door.

The best method of teaching your dog to behave in an acceptable fashion while inside the house is to pick moments when you are doing nothing more than watching television or reading a book. A blanket or rug should be put in a specific place so that the dog will learn that this is his area of the house. Ideally, this is located next to your favourite chair where you spend time sitting still. Preferably the dog would have had his daily walk, even his evening meal so it is now time for a little relaxation, which is what would be typical if the dog lived in the wild within a pack. Bring the dog in on a collar and lead, and make him sit on the bedding, then pull his front legs forward so that he is unable to bear weight on them, forcing him to lie down. At the same time, give the command to 'drop'. Once in the down position, very gently stroke the dog. Do not make a big fuss of him as this will make him excited and cause him to stand up. After two to four days of doing this, say, 'on your bed' as he is about to step onto his bed and then tell him to 'drop'.

Within two weeks, your dog will learn that not only does he have a place in your heart but he also has a specific place in your house. Your dog has also learnt two new commands: one is 'on your bed', the other is to 'drop' when he is told. Once the dog has learned this, it's a good idea to have him lie next to you while you are having your dinner. This should always be done before the dog eats, teaching him that you and your family are the pack leaders and there is a specific behaviour he must follow while he is in your house.

The dog should be comfortable while on his bed and should not need to get up and walk around. If he does, providing he is on the lead, you can simply correct him saying 'back on your bed', 'drop' and give him a pat for the correct behaviour. Positive reinforcement is the key to any successful long-term learning program.

If you happen to be sitting on your chair reading a book that you just cannot put down, don't forget your dog might need a toilet break or a drink of water while you are sipping your coffee.

This simple exercise will teach your dog many desired behaviours and develop an incredible bond between you both. It will also show that learning is an enjoyable experience, resulting in praise rather than reprimand.

16. Is there a foolproof way to toilet-train my dog?

Toilet-training for inside and outside the home should commence the first day the dog is brought home. Think dog! This catch-cry is bandied around by all good dog trainers and fits best in the toilet-training scenario. You must observe your dog carefully and know when it wants to go to the toilet. In most cases this isn't too difficult.

Puppies will want to relieve their bladders at specific times: when they wake up, after a meal and after a play. At these times, you should place your pup on the area you have assigned for going to the toilet. Don't play with the pup, just allow nature to take its course. As the pup relieves itself use the word 'toilet' (or what ever verbal command you wish to use — my wife prefers 'puddles') and praise the dog as it goes to the toilet. 'Good dog, toilet, good dog'. For a while, these are just noises to your dog but soon it associates your words and pleasant attitude with the fact that it is relieving itself. Police dogs are trained in this fashion so they will toilet on command rather than stopping in the middle of a building search or while apprehending a criminal!

Of course, accidents will happen so be prepared. Learn your dog's mannerisms and postures before it goes to the toilet. If you see it 'assuming the position', take it out immediately, then wait for it to relieve itself. As it does, don't forget that word along with praise.

For those occasions when you haven't been sufficiently diligent and a puddle or worse is happening on your carpet, admonish the animal with the word no and carry it outside. If the job has already been completed on your floor then by all means grumble in front of your dog while you're cleaning it up. Most people will tell you that it's too late to admonish the dog once it has gone to the toilet inside the house. Nonsense! Dogs are not stupid, they can smell the fact that the excrement you're grumbling about belongs to them.

When cleaning up after your dog, do not use ammonia detergents or disinfectants. These will smell similar to another animal's urine so your dog will be tempted to compete with this smell by covering it up with another urine sample. The best agents to use are those that repel a dog: citronella-based disinfectants, eucalyptus and tea-tree oil.

These disinfectants can also be diluted to spray on the areas of the yard where you do not want the dog to soil. Dogs can be taught to toilet in one area, especially if the smell on the ground tells them they have emptied themselves there before. Like people, dogs don't like going to the toilet where they eat and sleep, so keep these areas apart.

Now what about that stubborn dog who poos all over the yard — can anything be done? Yes, but this is getting tricky. You need a soft collar, a lead, a box of matches and some petroleum jelly. After a meal or a rest, put the dog on a collar and lead, take one match out from the box, place some petroleum jelly on the wooden end and, lifting your dog's tail, introduce it halfway into the anus. Let half the match just hang out and walk the dog around in the area you've selected for going to the toilet. The match in the anus will stimulate a bowel motion, and all the while you're saying 'toilet, good dog, toilet.'

Remember, the rules you must follow are consistency, persistence and patience.

17. Can you really teach a dog not to bark?

If you mean teach a dog to never, ever bark, the answer is a resounding no. For thousands of years, humans have selected dogs that bark. The first meeting of humans and dogs was not an accident. Dogs had probably been following nomadic tribes for many years. Those tribes would allow these scavengers to feed from their scraps and bones, and would feel safe knowing the pack would bark at the threat of intruders. Even today, when many people buy a dog they often ask if it will bark if strangers come near their house.

It is possible to prevent nuisance barking, providing the owners are prepared to take certain steps to change the environment and routine for their dog. Dogs most commonly bark because they are bored. Exercise is an ideal way to distract them from boredom and having to amuse themselves. But this doesn't always work. An extension of physical activity is mental exercise, so once a week obedience classes, with five to twenty minutes daily practice becomes a vital routine to avoid overt barking behaviour.

An unusual exercise that dogs can be taught is to bark on command. Dogs that learn this will often not bark excessively, only raising a noise when it's absolutely necessary or when given a command to do so by their owner.

The place where the dog lives needs to be closely examined. If a dog has a view to passing pedestrians or passing dogs, it might bark either to greet these other animals or to warn them he is on duty and not to come around again. Either way, the dog quickly develops the habit of excess barking. A blind on a side area may make all the difference to a dog's barking patterns.

And while you're looking at the yard, think seriously about building a maze for your pooch. A tunnel, an elevated platform (it only needs be a little way off the ground), even some of the hard plastic garden toys for children can assist in building a more interesting environment for your dog. There are many toys that can amuse dogs for hours. One of the best is called a Kong. You place food inside it and the dog then spends much of its day trying to get the food out, using tongue and teeth to eventually source all the hidden treasures inside the rubber device. The dog will learn to bounce it around on a hard surface to assist with the extraction of the food and for the simple amusement of watching it bounce.

Telling the dog to be quiet can work, but when you're not at home the dog will go along merrily barking, as no one is there to correct it. If discipline is to be effective, it needs to work without the dog being aware of how it happened. Hide hoses in strategic locations (or a kid's giant water soaker), leave home, and make sure the dog sees you but then double back without being seen. When the dog barks, hit it from the edge of a building or fence with a squirt of water and try not to let the dog see you.

If you're going to yell, do it when the dog least expects it and only use one word. Learn to growl the preferred word at the dog, just as its mother or the pack leader would if they were displeased with the dog. Whenever my dogs perform an unacceptable behaviour, I growl a resounding no. It doesn't matter what word you choose but be consistent and never use long sentences. Just a sharp, stern word.

Do not be consistent with the place or time you admonish your dog for barking. If you only yell at the dog from the side window or only when you're home from work then the dog will avoid the side window or bark whenever you're not home. You can tape your voice saying the special word and have someone play it to your dog when the pooch is misbehaving and you are out.

Another idea is to use high frequency noise emitters. You can't hear them but your dog can. A nuisance barker can be taught to stop barking every time it hears such a sound and you can supply a couple to the neighbours for times when you're not at home.

A very good friend asked me if I'd authorise him to use an electric collar to stop his dog barking. I refused. No dog needs an electric collar to beat him up every time he barks.

Electric collars do work but the reality is that you don't need violence to train a dog not to bark, because there are plenty of other options to consider — unless maybe you're not as smart as the dog.

18. Can a backyard really be made escape-proof?

You can make a yard escape-proof providing you have a higher IQ than your dog.

Think: how can your dog escape and why does your dog want to escape? The most common method of escape is through an open gate. This is especially seen during school holidays, which is also the most common period for dogs to be hit by cars.

The solution is simple: spring-shutting, self-bolting gates. These are often utilised around pool areas to prevent children from having unsupervised access. These gates are ideal to prevent the dog from escaping and also afford some peace of mind when children are in the backyard and you need to be inside.

The athletic jumper can pose a problem, as some of the working-type dogs see a high fence as a challenge. Dogs can scale extremely high fences so some smart construction work is required to address this problem. The top of the fence requires an additional fixture that leans in towards the backyard. As the dog attempts to scale the fence, it is confronted by a physical barrier at the top, which would require the dog to jump on the full rather than skimming up the fence. The jump is impossible so the dog remains secure. To stop your yard looking like a prison compound, try hanging pots or training vines along the fence.

The only other method of escape, apart from breaking the fence down (and that only reflects bad engineering), is to dig under the fence. The digging dog can easily be secured in the yard but it requires a little work. Wire mesh, dug about 30 to 40 cm into the ground and attached to the fence will discourage most diggers. The gate area can be a potential problem but wire dug down with a little concrete track on top would foil most dogs' attempt at escape.

You need to consider why a dog would wish to leave its own yard.

In the case of male dogs, the scent of a bitch in season or on heat would be sufficient stimulus for them to plan an escape. If you are not going to breed from your dog, de-sexing should be given serious consideration and is an absolute must if the animal is a repeat escapee.

Dogs enjoy company. They are by nature a pack animal and love most of all to be with the pack leader. Dogs hate being locked in a yard, not receiving the contact and stimulation they deserve. There are three things you should do if you own a dog:

- Take it for daily walks.
- Give it some quality time indoors with you.
- Take it to obedience classes.

Obedience classes especially help with socialisation with other dogs and other people. If you're not providing at least two of these three comforts for your dog, you need to consider whether or not you are a suitable owner.

19. How can I stop my dog destroying the backyard?

In case you haven't noticed it by now, dogs are basically intelligent and gregarious. The first species to be domesticated, they enjoy the company of people. In fact, many dogs prefer being with humans rather than their own species. Left alone, boredom can set in and this can result in unacceptable or nuisance behaviour, requiring the offending animal to undergo extensive retraining. Unless, of course, you look after your dog's interests.

When a dog bonds strongly with a person who fails to teach that dog tolerance and patience, certain consequences must be expected when the two become separated. Some dogs will simply sulk around until their owner returns, while others become anxious to be reunited. A dog that is continually left alone will find its own entertainment and stimulation. It might start pulling clothes off the line or knocking pot plants off window-sills, or digging up the garden. Dogs require both physical and mental stimulation in order to avoid boredom. A dog that has been on an exhausting run with its owner is less likely to develop the habit of incessant barking compared with a dog that is continually confined to its yard. Allowing a dog to roam by itself outside the yard is not an option – it's irresponsible and dangerous and teaches the dog independence to the point where it cannot distinguish acceptable behaviour.

Teaching your dog tolerance and patience should begin on the first day the puppy enters your house. An easily cleaned, sheltered, quiet area of your house needs to allotted as the puppy's area of confinement. This may be a laundry area inside the house, a kennel and pen in the backyard or a small wire enclosure where the puppy can be safely confined. Your dog needs to spend short periods in the selected area where it may be fed a bone to give it a distraction from its solitude. Under no circumstances should the animal be attended to while it is barking or whining for attention. Prior to having placed the puppy in the pen, you should take the dog outside, have a small play and give it ample opportunity to go to the toilet.

Mental stimulation for your dog can be provided in a few ways. A concentrated ten minute obedience lesson goes a long way to providing mental exercise for the pooch. To ensure that this is delivered effectively you will need to be committed to weekly obedience school where a qualified instructor can teach you how to correctly train your animal.

Leaving a large bone with your dog can assist in the initial separation anxiety experienced by the animal, but depending upon the size of the bone and the effectiveness of the dog's teeth, this distraction may be short-lived. Toys can also assist in providing amusement to the dog and generally should be utilised at two particular times. Firstly, the owner should encourage play behaviour with the toys during fun times in the backyard and secondly, offer the toys for the dog to play with when you are leaving the house. See page 55 for more information on toys for your dog.

If your dog is destructive whenever you are away from home, it is a matter of going right back to basics and beginning the lessons from scratch. You will need to spend money on a secure and safe pen that prevents your dog from accessing areas where it creates the greatest amount of damage in your yard. Next you will need to allow your dog to see you while it is confined in its pen. So make the pen an attractive area for the dog by playing games or feeding the animal in its new confined area.

The pen, or in fact any yard, can be enhanced both aesthetically and for the dog's amusement by the use of blinds and mazes. An attractive panel bordered by fast growing shrubs or with a water feature in the centre can be decorative while providing the dog with a more interesting environment. Converting such a partition into a more complex maze can enhance the area further for the dog because it then sees the yard as having many different areas for it to investigate. You can then hide small portions of food or toys in different areas within the yard, affording the animal rewards during its solitary, investigative hours.

There are quite a few reasons why dogs dig. Looking at it from the dog's point of view, digging is considered normal. In fact, when a dog digs in a freshly worked garden bed, it is simply mimicking your behaviour. It's seen you till the soil and is just helping you out. Worse still, if you add compost or fertiliser to the garden bed (especially in the form of blood and bone) the area is all the more inviting.

One important factor in trying to understand a dog's digging behaviour is that some breeds are actually meant to dig. The word 'terrier' for example, comes from the Latin word that means 'to hide', and terriers are literally dogs that go to ground. Terriers will burrow into small holes digging their way in to find their prey. Dogs will also do this in very hot weather in an attempt to create a cooler environment. Making a den to sleep in is not unnatural for any dog.

Rather than embarking on a major construction project to build a den, many dogs dig at random, leaving potholes throughout the backyard. This behaviour is usually attributed to the release of pent-up energy and these dogs dig for the sheer enjoyment and exercise value. Geriatric dogs lose some ability to regulate their body temperature, often feeling the cold or the heat much more than when they were younger. In these cases, old dogs start digging to find a more comfortable environment, perhaps even digging when they are indoors, which has disastrous results for the carpet. Finally, some dogs dig simply because they are deprived of social contact with people. Dogs will dig near gates or doors or any area where people may congregate — the dog is attempting to escape its solitary confinement and is simply looking for attention, especially from humans.

Try to study your dog's digging behaviour so that the cause may be properly assessed. This is important in establishing the best method for treatment.

The hardest digging behaviour to treat is that which arises because of genetic predisposition. While inherited (or innate) behaviour can be changed, it is so entrenched in some animals that any change may be short-lived unless it is continually reinforced. For dogs that dig because it is in their nature, the most effective therapy is allowing them to find a distraction from the digging. Structured obedience classes with lessons given by you to your dog each day may provide mental stimulation to change the dog's behaviour to some extent. Toys left in the backyard may also help, providing the dog doesn't get in the habit of wanting to bury them

Alternatively, you can hide around the corner with a hose and each time the dog starts to dig, squirt it with water. This gives the animal a negative response to the digging behaviour. The dog should never know that you are causing the jet of water.

Many dogs will dig repeatedly in the same area so, if you find holes appearing in a regular spot, try setting mouse traps in the freshly dug dirt. Small mouse traps are not sufficient to cause any damage to your animal but springing them accidentally will often startle a dog and deter them from digging. While these methods do not work in every case, when they do produce the desired effect the results are often very gratifying and long-lasting.

Dogs that enjoy digging simply to release energy obviously require therapy. If you spend fifteen to thirty minutes once or twice each day throwing a ball, the bursts of energy required for sprinting will soon tire the animal.

Dogs that enjoy digging because you have produced a fresh garden bed for them require this environment to be made more hostile. You need to invest in a few cans of red-hot cayenne pepper, sprinkling it in large quantities in the freshly dug soil. While this may seem somewhat cruel, red cayenne pepper can be utilised as a negative reinforcement for many undesirable behaviours, such as discouraging the dog from placing his head in the rubbish bin. If you have spent a few hours preparing a flowerbed, the cayenne pepper is probably far kinder than tying the dog up or confining it to an extremely small run.

For dogs that dig to improve the quality of their resting place, good bedding and an insulated kennel with shade and proper cooling will assist greatly. A good kennel can be equivalent to providing the dog with a den-like region, thus negating the need for digging either to improve its environment, or in an inherited desire to construct its own house.

Many people have tried things like filling the hole with the dog's own faeces or filling it with water. If all else fails, then it is worth a try. However trainers have not found great success with either of these techniques. If nothing appears to work you may need to build a concrete or paved area for the dog to confine it when you are not at home.

20. How can I stop my dog being aggressive?

If a dog is overtly dominant, it may be ready to discipline a human by delivering a bite. Therefore, as its owner, there are some difficult issues you must face. If you have a child in the family you could be in serious trouble. The dog will see the child as a subordinate pack member so if, in the dog's opinion, the child acts incorrectly (perhaps holding up a toy) then the dog may react by biting the child. Over 50 per cent of dog bites to children are delivered by the family dog!

If you have an aggressive dog and it seems possible that your dog will bite a child, you need to consider euthanasia of the dog as a possible action before the bite takes place. Harsh words. Harsher actions. But you must seriously consider all the options when dealing with an aggressive dog.

Training of an aggressive dog requires the owner to take charge of the dog, planting themselves firmly at the top of the pack. In fact, the dog must not only become a subordinate to the owner/trainer of the family but also needs to realise it is of no higher stature in the pack than any family member. Formal training allows the dog to learn the correct response to any command, especially the 'drop' or 'down' command. Making the dog lie down has the animal assume the second most submissive position. The most submissive position would have the dog lie down rolling onto its back exposing the neck and under-belly. This position is difficult to teach so simply having the dog drop flat when told will be sufficient in attempting to reverse aggression. An aggressive dog should be taught to remain in that position until released by the handler. 'Drop and stay' is vital and easily taught.

The training method must be firm, with the handler always in control. Usually, methods involving soft collars will not achieve results with a large, dominant dog. A correctly utilised check chain or a 'halti' will be needed to ensure control and achieve results.

You must always be in control during training and be in a position that allows you to make the dog complete the exercise once you have issued the command. And a command it is. With a dominant or aggressive dog, never ask it to fulfil an exercise. The sequence must always be: command, correct action, praise. 'Correct action' will initially entail your firm but gentle intervention to ensure positive completion of the exercise, ending with praise.

Even while the dog is in the initial training phase, it should be brought inside on a lead during family mealtime. You should eat your meal at the table with your dog made to lie down beside you until all the family have finished. Then, and only then, do you feed the dog. As bottom of the pack, the dog is the last to eat.

To reinforce this pecking order, you go through the door first when you are carrying the dog's feed bowl outside, and then your dog follows. Every gate, every door, every opening or passage you should negotiate first, pulling your dog back if you have to, ensuring it follows.

Drugs can assist in calming an aggressive dog and your vet can advise you. Remember though, drugs alone cannot provide the answer and must be combined with a properly constructed training program.

In the case of an entire (not de-sexed) male then castration may assist in reducing aggression. There are other factors involved, such as correct socialisation and training, but testosterone in males does remain a factor affecting aggression. In aggressive males, de-sexing is often followed with the use of progesterone, a female hormone that often makes male dogs more mellow.

Part of the training program must involve socialisation. The dog should be out with you, meeting lots of new people. This doesn't mean you ask everyone to pat the dog. 'Meeting' can simply mean the dog lies at your side while lots of strangers pass by, so it learns that the presence of other people does not signify a danger. It certainly must not prompt the dog into any form of action.

When do you know all the training paid off? When the dog dies of old age and hasn't bitten anyone! When you own an aggressive dog you must always stay alert, paying extra attention when your dog is involved with people. Every dog owner should carry public risk insurance to cover themselves against their dog biting someone (see page 143), but it's all the more important for owners of an aggressive dog. Unfortunately, in some instances, euthanasia of the overtly aggressive dog is not an unreasonable resolution.

21. My dog is shy. What can I do to help it?

If you are the owner of a shy dog you need to realise that you own a potentially dangerous animal — a shy dog that is cornered is more dangerous than the most aggressive, dominant dog

Shyness in dogs is present for two reasons: genetics or a negative experience during development. Try to meet the parents before you buy a pup and be aware that certain breeds are known for their reserved nature. Environment plays a large role in the development of a dog's character and a bad experience can render a dog shy or fearful for the rest of its life. A lack of positive experiences during the early stages of life can also result in poor character development. Dogs need to be socialised with other dogs as well as humans and other animals.

If an owner notices that their dog is overly shy or reserved, steps need to be taken immediately to reverse the situation. If a particular event or specific scenario has resulted in the dog's shyness and the owner has identified this, then reconstruction of the event may assist in reversing a negative attitude. Prior to any work being done on the dog, however, the owner must have the dog's total trust and confidence.

There are two simple methods of achieving and improving the bond between dog and owner. Firstly, crouch next to your dog at feeding time, pat him and talk in a calm voice while he is eating. If the dog is allowed to sleep inside, then bonding can continue while you are relaxing watching TV or even while you are in bed asleep with the dog lying next to you (on the floor, of course). Secondly, regular walks are extremely beneficial to bonding as your dog feels he is on an adventure with you as the pack leader, ensuring his constant safety.

Some of the best areas to walk your dog when you are tying to socialise are busy locations where there are lots of humans and noises — outside a railway station at peak hour is ideal. Ensure that you are continually walking with your dog at a brisk pace, talking and reassuring him that all is well, constantly distracting him from the masses of people and noises that might otherwise frighten him. If this is done correctly and repeatedly your dog will soon learn to accommodate the noises and humans that would otherwise cause him irrational fear and grief.

You should also give the dog formal obedience lessons, instilling further confidence in you as his master. During obedience classes, the dog will meet people who understand dogs and how they think. These people will occasionally run their hands over your dog but only when you have told your dog to 'stay', ensuring he only focuses on you. If your dog fails to stay, becoming too terrified of the stranger patting and handling him, then further distractions in the form of food or toys may be required.

Medication can be used to calm the dog down, when normal training methods fail, or in an attempt to shortcut or assist training. If you intend to use a herbal preparation, choose one based on valerian which has a calming, sedating effect. Be prepared to wait at least six weeks as they can take time to work.

If all this still doesn't relieve your dog's shyness then it may be time to seek professional help. Your vet might discuss referral to a behavioural specialist or raise the option of drug therapy. Clomipramine is registered for use in dogs, assisting in such conditions as separation anxiety, aggression and shyness. Drugs alone will not assist and must be used in conjunction with training methods designed to correct the problem.

In any canine training program it's the small steps that count. Never expect your shy dog to accept the most onerous of challenges, and discuss the program you set for the animal with a competent trainer. And remember, your attention, presence and praise combined with repeated situations will give the dog confidence in itself and in you.

20. How can I stop my dog being carsick?

Carsickness or motion illness is usually a problem in dogs that aren't used to travelling in cars. The easiest method of teaching your dog to enjoy the car is to drive your dog around the block every day then play with it for five minutes. Taking the dog for a daily ride helps it cope with the motion of a car and playing with the dog afterwards gives it a positive reinforcement of the experience.

The whole process can be made easier if you plan ahead. Ginger travel sickness tablets, available at a health food shops or chemists, do work well in dogs but you need to give them at least thirty minutes before travelling.

Your vet can supply drugs that stop vomiting (anti-emetics) but these do not always work. For an instant fix, a mild tranquilliser or sedative can be of assistance. This is especially beuful in dogs that suddenly have to be relocated long distances by land or air travel. The tranquilliser not only stops sickness but also calms the dog down, removing fear of the many unknown noises that the dog will hear. Acetylpromazine (ACP) is the most common tranquilliser for this purpose because it is reasonably long acting but still safe. It cannot be used in boxers as they are extremely sensitive to this drug, which drops their blood pressure to dangerously low levels.

Given the opportunity to learn to travel in cars, dogs can actually enjoy it.

23. What is rage syndrome?

Some twenty years ago, I was watching a class of dogs being judged at one of the country's largest dog shows. A new import in springer spaniels was being exhibited and I was interested to see how this dog would fare. The handler, an experienced man, was standing the dog in position when suddenly the dog erupted like a volcano. Barking, snarling, snapping and biting the handler, the dog entered an irrational, overtly aggressive phase which probably lasted no more than one minute. In this brief time, it had managed to inflict several wounds that, although damaging, could have been worse in the hands of a less experienced trainer. These moments of unpredictable aggression are referred to as 'rage syndrome' and have been seen in other breeds such as the English cocker spaniel, Saint Bernard, Bernese mountain dog, border collie and some of the terrier breeds.

Some dogs display disorientation, trembling, even urination and defecation while having this episode of unpredictable, severe aggression. Once the moment has passed the dog quickly returns to normal without realising the damage it may have inflicted — it is as though there has been a moment of total mental blackout.

Many breeders will defend their breeds, saying that it is likely to be dominance aggression or some other form of irrational behaviour in individuals. Regardless, if there are sporadic bouts of irrational aggressive behaviour within any breed, close scrutiny for possible inheritance of this behaviour is important. Dogs that display aggressive behaviour for whatever reason should not be used in breeding programs and their bloodlines should not be promoted.

Treatment for dogs with rage syndrome can be difficult and needs to be seriously considered as the safety of humans must be of primary concern. Your vet can prescribe various drugs including behavioural modifiers, anti-epileptic drugs and even hormone regimes. If the dog lives in the household with children present at any time then euthanasia is not an unreasonable consideration.

24. My dog is petrified of thunderstorms. What can I do?

Fear of thunderstorms is not uncommon in dogs and can even occur in the group of dogs called gun dogs. This group of dogs can work in the field to retrieve or flush game while the owner hunts with a very loud shotgun, yet can still can be frightened by thunder.

It is obviously more than the loud cracking noise of the thunder that can bring fear and irrational terror to the hearts of our canine companions. Dogs who are scared of thunderstorms have been known to jump through plate glass windows, severely damaging themselves. Other dogs have torn at fences or back doors not only damaging the structure but also their feet and nails.

Dogs can tell when a storm is approaching in two ways. The obvious one is from the sound of thunder rolling through the valleys or off mountains many miles away, but the other way is far more intriguing. They can actually feel, or are attuned to, the drop in barometric air pressure associated with the oncoming storm.

Humans, too, have the ability to detect the change in air pressure but we are so out of tune with our senses, relying on technology and weather reports, that few of us ever realise that our bodies have such potential. Fewer of us ever train our bodies to further develop these senses, preferring to vaguely call it a 'sixth' sense when it comes into play at odd times.

Behavioural specialists will tell you that such animals have to be taught to 'accommodate' thunderstorms. To achieve this, they have recorded tapes and videos of thunderstorms, which are placed on a very low volume with the animal nearby. As the dog learns to ignore or accommodate the soft noise of the thunderstorm, this is slowly increased in volume. The process continues until the dog can remain inside the room next to speakers that are blaring out the sounds of the thunderstorm at full blast. Some dogs develop a fear of thunderstorms as a result of the owner's fear. While the taped thunder does not cause any fear to the owner and such a tape can allow a dog to learn to accommodate the noise, when a real thunderstorm hits, the dog cannot turn to the owner for reassurance because the owner is afraid.

One problem with thunderstorms is that they may occur when the owner is not at home to bring the dog inside and reassure it. The dog's frantic behaviour may cause damage either to itself or to the surroundings. Obviously, owners should not punish the destructive behaviour that can cause a tearing down of a door or breaking of a window, but they should not spend time reassuring the dog either, as this only rewards that behaviour. Owners should remain neutral when they find the dog in a frantic irrational state due to a storm.

Dogs often know a storm is coming before it hits, and this is when they may commence their frantic or destructive behaviour. At this time, the dog should be placed somewhere safe and, if possible, soundproof. Using thick foam panels, such as those used for insulation of cool rooms, owners can build a reasonably sound proof kennel for their pet. The door should be in the form of a maze so that it need not be shut and will allow the dog to enter and leave as it needs. When a storm is coming, the dog should be tranquillised, then placed inside the kennel area along with a reassuring blanket or towel with the owner's scent.

One owner built such a kennel for his dog and placed a radio at low volume inside. Inside the kennel the noise of the radio functioned in two ways. Firstly, it provided human voices to distract from anything that was going on outside, thereby giving the dog reassurance. Secondly, it created sufficient noise so that many claps of thunder could not be heard over the sound of the radio.

Successful treatments for desensitising a dog to thunderstorms aim at controlling the problem because complete elimination is usually impossible. Desensitisation can be difficult for dogs that cannot stand even the slightest noise that resembles a clap of thunder. Try playing a game where the dog tears up a paper bag. After a while the paper bag can be blown up, but still allow the dog to tear it up without any loud noises. Eventually the paper bag full of air should be exploded releasing the loud noise, and then offer the paper to the dog as a play article.

This type of therapy requires a very committed owner. When all these efforts fail, then the only reasonable way to assist the dog during a thunderstorm is to use a quick-acting tranquilliser. Drugs that take half an hour to take effect might not be of much value as the storm has often passed by the time the drug has taken effect. Acteylpromazine (ACP) is often prescribed but the tablets can take twenty minutes to have an effect. One trick that works is to crush the tablets, dissolve the powder in warm water and squirt it down the dog's mouth. The onset of action can be less than five minutes. Some dogs become so badly affected by thunderstorms that vets will teach owners how to administer a tranquillising injection so that the animal will simply sleep through a storm.

25. How do I stop my dog chasing his tail?

Whether or not you can get a positive response to therapy for tail-chasing depends largely on the cause of this behaviour. Fortunately, most dogs only go through the action of chasing their tail, but some do actual physical damage to themselves when they bite down hard into their own flesh.

Some dogs can be trained out of tail-chasing while others, despite the pain they inflict upon themselves, continue with self-mutilation until the only answer for the owner is to amputate the dog's tail. Often these types of tail-chases are genetically driven — there is good evidence that bull-terriers tail-chase because of a genetic origin. In bull-terriers the condition is sometimes linked with hydrocephalus (fluid or water on the brain). In such cases, treatment for hydro-cephalus can be attempted in order to minimise the tail chasing behaviour, but totally negating it will probably be impossible.

In some cases, the cause of tail-chasing is epilepsy and the abnor-mal behaviour indicates a seizure. In this case, anti-epileptic drugs work reasonably well and the behaviour is often controllable.

Sometimes purchasing the wrong breed for your backyard can lead to the animal to developing tail-chasing behaviour. Very active breeds that are confined to small yards and rarely exercised will start tail-chasing simply to release energy. Increasing both mental and physical activity can be effective in controlling this behaviour. If tail-chasing has become too ingrained into the animal's own psyche, the dog may require some form of drug therapy.

If drugs are used in conjunction with training and exercise then very positive responses can be expected, so that after a period of time the dog can be left drug-free without tail-chasing. In such animals, it is a very good idea to substitute one type of behaviour for another. For example, if the dog enjoys chasing a ball, when you see it chasing its tail, bounce a ball nearby to attract its attention and distract it from the undesirable behaviour. Alternatively, you can commence some form of obedience work, praising it as each exercise is completed, thus distracting it from its initial intent to tail-chase. This can go a long way towards settling your dog and allowing it to develop as a normal individual.

26. Is it better to have one or two dogs?

Whenever people ask about buying two puppies I always suggest that they buy them from different litters and that they purchase puppies of the opposite sex. In fact, I much prefer that people do not buy puppies of the same age and that they purchase them at least twelve months apart.

The answer to whether to own a single dog or more depends upon several factors. Firstly, the sex of the pair and whether they are de-sexed or not is important. While animals of the same sex can be trained to get along together without any disputes, it is generally agreed that a pair of dogs of the opposite sex are far less likely to fight. Secondly, age is a factor. As animals of the same age grow, they hit critical times of development simultaneously. During these periods, they may wish to test themselves out and what may have started as a friendly tussle will end up in a full-blown fight, possibly causing a lifelong resentment towards each other. Thirdly, dogs are pack animals and even a pair can form a pack. As a pack, they may resent interference or reprimands from any other animal or person outside the duo. A child entering a backyard which is the territory of two dogs can find itself in severe danger. When two dogs mount an attack, the effects can be devastating as they compete and egg each other on.

The breed of dog makes a big difference to whether or not to own two dogs. Certain breeds have much stronger instincts to pack and when they do, primitive behaviours tend to follow. Siberian huskies, basenjis, Alaskan Malamutes, some terriers and many of the dogs in the hound group will tend to quickly form packs. Dominant breeds develop strong territorial bonds, pushing each other on to defend their boundaries when there is more than one dog present. Rottweilers, German shepherds, Dobermans and cattle dogs are typical of the breeds with dominant temperaments.

If you own a dog that has been easy to train, has a fully developed temperament and is mature, then bringing in a second dog can be an advantage. You should still purchase a puppy not a mature or even adolescent animal as this can only result in challenges to the older dog. While you will still need to spend some time training your new puppy, it will actually mimic the behaviour of its older, more domi-nant canine companion, which makes training your new puppy so much easier.

If your mature animal is not de-sexed and is a pedigree, you could consider finding a suitable partner whose owner may wish to breed with your dog. Genetics is the obvious advantage that would flow on, as temperament has a very large genetic component. Having an offspring from your animal helps prepare you for the time when your much-loved dog dies.

The final decision as to whether to own one or two dogs is very complex. Your ability to train both animals so that their behaviours suit your lifestyle is vital so you must give due consideration to the amount of time that you are prepared to commit to your dogs.

27. Can a dog and a cat get on?

We have all heard the expression 'fight like cats and dogs', but while they are natural enemies, there are many instances where correct training allows cats and dogs to live happily in a family environment. There is no doubt that the best time to socialise a dog with a cat is during the early weeks of life, especially between three and twelve weeks of age. This is not to say that older dogs cannot be trained to socialise with cats or any other species for that matter. It simply means the younger the dog the easier the socialisation process becomes.

If you haven't purchased your dog or cat but you know you want one of each, breed selection is important. In the case of the dog, a sedate animal that can be easily trained and has already been well socialised makes an ideal partner for your household and the addition of a feline friend. The quieter dogs such as labradors, golden retrievers and cocker spaniels easily fit this picture. Many of the working dogs, because of their desire to please their owner, will not have an adverse reaction to a cat in the family. It can be difficult to introduce puppies to cats because their over-exuberance might find them fleeing in the wrong direction as a result of a swipe on the nose from the cat. However, the dog might respect the cat for this behaviour, providing of course it doesn't make the dog angry so that it wants to retaliate.

Within our household, dogs and cats happily accept each other's presence but are always introduced in an environment of absolute control. Puppies learn to live with cats as soon as they are weaned from their mother. At any time, the cat can jump onto a higher perch, escaping over-exuberant playing by the puppy. At the same time, if the puppy continues to chase the cats, it is quickly held and verbally admonished for this undesirable behaviour. In this way, all our dogs have learned to accept cats in the household with one female German shepherd even mothering two orphan kittens, which assisted in their rearing. It was just as well she made friends with them when they were so little as, being Bengal tigers, they were always going to outgrow her. Even when they were twice the size of the German shepherd they would do her no harm, even during rough play.

If you already own a dog and wish to introduce a cat into the household it is very important that the dog be both tested and socialised with cats prior to the purchase of a new kitten. Many people do live with cats and dogs and you need to find a friend that has a socialised feline or you may wish to make enquiries at your local dog training school. Your dog must be placed on a collar and lead that allows it to be under proper control at all times and it must never be able to slip its collar. You should have sufficient control to instruct your dog to sit quietly and accept the presence of the cat. If you have no control over your dog, consider having some private obedience lessons, continuing until your dog reliably sits, drops and heels when it is told. A reliable dog should lie down when it is told and have no desire to leave even when the cat is passing by.

It is important to realise that if you have the wrong breed, or a dog that has not been properly socialised during the first three months of its life, it could be far safer not to introduce a cat into the household. However, all dogs, even those that have been trained to kill cats, can be desensitised through a long training process. It will require commitment on your part, combined with patience and persistence. In the initial training period, the animals should be separated by a firm wire mesh fence for the protection of everyone, especially the cat. This is not training that should be undertaken at home if your dog is focused on destroying the cat. Rather, you should seek the help of professional trainers so that your animal can be reliably taught to live in harmony with a feline friend.

28. My dog is too fat. Should I put him on a diet?

People come into my clinic all the time with overweight dogs and I try to convince them of their dog's problem. 'Hey, I should charge you two consultation fees,' I tell them. 'After all you've got two dogs in one skin!' Or a little more subtle, 'Oh, what a novel idea, you've got a moving coffee table!'

Many owners reply by saying, 'I just haven't been able to exercise him as much lately.' Or you really know that the dog is in trouble when they ask, 'You don't really think he's that fat, do you?' The biggest part of the problem is the owner. If the owner admits their dog is too fat, then the problem can be addressed. If not, then the dog will die sooner rather than later.

One of the longest pet food studies ever conducted was by a dog food manufacturer in the USA. Two large groups of dogs were tested. One group was fed as much food as they wanted. Many of these dogs were labradors so you can imagine how much they ate. No dogs were allowed to become so overweight that they would unduly suffer, but many were the weight of the average size pet at home. The second group were fed two-thirds of the amount eaten by the first group. These dogs were thinner, some might even say skinny, but none ever became so thin that they were unhealthy. The outcome of the study was that not only were the thinner dogs were much more active but they all outlived the dogs in the fat group by many years.

If you're not sure whether your dog is overweight talk to your vet, ask some experienced breeders and check some references about your breed of dog.

Before embarking on any weight reduction program for a fat dog, you need to make certain that the animal's obesity doesn't stem from a disease such as a poorly performing thyroid gland. A low-acting thyroid (hypothyroidism) leads to obesity, lethargy, and hair loss.

Assuming your dog has no health problems, obesity occurs simply because of too much food. De-sexed dogs do have a lower metabolism and tend to lay fat under the skin quickly, but this just reflects too many calories going down the gullet.

So how do we diet the overweight dog without starving the poor animal? Answer: change foods. There are commercial foods that are labelled 'lite', which means they have fewer calories. However, you must still follow the feeding instructions on the packet and never give any tasty titbits.

Alternatively, you can feed the dog a homemade diet. Mix cooked cabbage, zucchini, marrow and squash with a little lean mince or even some canned food. For a large breed of dog, feed the dog no more than 150 g of meat, for a medium size breed, feed no more than 100 g of meat and for a small dog, feed 20 to 50 g of meat. Do not include any other vegetables, rice or pasta. This is low in calories, high in roughage and very filling. Your dog still feels loved and you can be happy in the knowledge that you're filling the dog's tummy with fewer calories and it will therefore lose weight.

Exercise will raise your dog's metabolic rate but the single most important thing is fewer calories. Weigh your dog each fortnight so you can monitor its weight loss.

It's important to realise that a 30 kg dog that should weigh 25 kg is 20 per cent overweight. Five kilos overweight doesn't sound like much but imagine what you would be like if you were carrying an extra 20 per cent in weight.

29. What is the best dog food?

Dog owners can easily become confused by the range of products on the pet food shelves. Some of the label claims would have us believe that, to a dog, a particular brand is like a three course meal, including all the nutritional attributes super-vitamins, balanced in every mineral, amino acid, carbohydrate and any other food parameter the advertisers can think to mention. What are we to believe?

Pet food manufacturers spend millions of dollars on research to capture part of the pet food market that is worth billions of dollars. One company performs over one million scientific recordings each year and has large research farms dedicated to producing better dog foods. Their work has been rewarded with the development of super-premium dog food. These products are far more expensive but some of them are even better than any food you could make at home.

Are super-premium products really necessary? No, dogs can and do survive on old-fashioned dog food but it's the same as feeding a person rice with occasional protein compared to a balanced diet with fruit, meat, cereals, dairy products, minerals and, of course ice-cream. Well, maybe not ice-cream although it should be a food group of its own, just like chocolate cake!

There are many companies now that manufacture their own brand of super-premium product without the research to back up their claims so you must be cautious as to what brands you purchase. The imitation brands don't have the resources to produce foods that are in the same class as the super-premium products but the writing on the label would have you believe they do.

The other area that needs to be addressed is that of 'natural' diets. The worst of these makes the outlandish statement that it is natural Dogs in the wild will occasionally eat a whole animal, usually a herbivore of some kind. Dogs kill in packs, taking down bigger herbivores and the first area that is consumed is certainly not raw meaty bones. Rather, they eat the abdominal contents containing the intestines, which are full of vegetable matter that is cooked inside the herbivore's intestinal tract. The abdominal region is also highest in fat, containing such organs as the kidneys and the liver. Feeding raw vegetables and meaty bones is not only unnatural but can be harmful. Old dogs have great difficulties digesting these so constipation, especially in males that may have prostatitis, is a serious side effect.

If you do elect to avoid commercial food, do so properly. Cook cereals such as pasta and rice, add some fresh, fatty meat and remember to add some extra calcium and vitamins especially for very young pups.

Raw bones should be given to every dog but not as a major part of the diet. Raw brisket bones or mutton flaps are ideal because the dog needs to really use its teeth to crack, crush and tear these down to small pieces. Gums and teeth benefit enormously from this activity. You can avoid expensive veterinary bills for cleaning the dog's teeth under anaesthetic every couple of years. See pages 136 for more information on looking after your dog's teeth. Keeping the gums clean will also avoid bacterial build up, maintaining fresh breath.

An important word about feeding raw meaty bones to dogs: make sure they are raw. Cooking bones changes the matrix, making them indigestible so they have to pass through as whole pieces. Often they can block the digestive tract or even pierce through the intestine. Many people will feed their dogs cooked bones and never have a problem, but cooked bones have been known to cause problems, and the situation is easily avoided.

Leftovers can be an enjoyable variation for your dog but be cautious as some dogs have very sensitive tummies — sudden changes or additions to their diet may lead to diarrhoea or, worse still, bloat. Avoid spicy or very salty food and never feed your dog large quantities of cooked onions. Also forget about giving dogs food that is off: fungal and bacterial infections can affect a dog just as much as a human.

A common mistake is to feed your dog lots of fresh meat. Meat, regardless of whether it's beef, lamb, chicken or fish is high in phosphorus. Dogs' blood must have a slightly higher calcium level than phosphorus to maintain correct muscle function and contraction. If the phosphorus level is suddenly too high, the muscles, including the heart, may not contract properly. The monitoring system of the body quickly corrects this problem by releasing calcium from the bones. The blood is satisfied, its mineral ratio is re-established; the calcium is again higher than the phosphorus. The muscles, especially the heart, are happy and continue doing their work. But the bones have lost calcium and become thinner, even weaker. If the situation continues, the bones can even fracture. Calcium supplements alone cannot offset this condition and a balanced diet is essential — never allow fresh meat to form a major component of a dog's diet.

The single most important consideration is to keep your dog lean. A study that spanned over a decade fed two groups of labradors for their entire lifetime. One group was fed as much as they wanted to eat, and being labradors, they quickly became overweight. The second group were all fed on restricted rations. These dogs had fewer defects and longer life spans. Further, dogs that are prone to genetic diseases such as hip dysplasia are more likely to develop symptoms if they are overweight.

When you purchase a new pup you should receive a diet chart. Ask for it well before you pick up the pup so that you can stock up on the products nominated in the diet. If you wish to change the food selected by the breeder, do so slowly but remember, you probably selected from this breeder because you liked the adult dogs they owned. Those dogs would have been fed on the food the breeder recommends so think carefully and have good reasons before changing diet.

Analyse this to work out what to feed your dog:

1   Is there always fresh, clean, cool water available for your dog?
2   Is your dog in a lean, sleek condition?
3   When you purchased your pup, were you given a diet chart that could be easily followed and are the recommended products readily accessible?
4   As your pup grows, does it have straight, strong legs with firm, tight feet, not splayed toes with excessively loose ligaments?
5   Does your dog enjoy the food you have selected as the main component in the diet?
6   Are you confident about the product you are feeding your dog?
7   Is there evidence of real, scientific research on the food you have decided upon for your pet?
8   Do you feed raw bones to your dog at least three times each week?
9   Is your dog's coat always shiny, displaying good coat quality that reflects correct levels of essential oils and vitamins in the diet?

It all depends how important your dog is to you and your family. Dogs can survive on very little but if you want to feed your dog properly then you should be able to answer yes to all of the above.

30. Can dogs be vegetarian?

While we tend to think of dogs in the wild as sleek, keen hunters, they are largely a scavenger pack. The pack hunts and kills together but they are also opportunistic scavengers feeding on whatever material they might find. They learned in the wild to dig up various root plants and to extract certain vitamins from plants and grass juices. However, dogs lack the ability to break down plant cells the way herbivores do. In the wild, the main form of vegetable matter they consume is found partially digested in the stomach and intestines of the herbivores they kill.

The dog's nutritional requirements are high during the first six months of its life. If you elect a vegetarian diet during this part of your dog's rearing, you need to consider the addition of some animal protein in the form of milk product, cheese or eggs. The absolute vegan who will not eat eggs and cheese may be asking too much of their dog if they offer only a vegan diet during the dog's rapid growth stage. Supplements must be considered, especially dolomite, a combination of calcium carbonate and magnesium, and a host of other minerals and vitamins to aid growth and metabolism.

One difficulty will be in giving sufficient good quality vegetable protein to your dog. Dogs do very well on carbohydrates, so rice and pasta can form the basis of their diet. Soya protein can be useful but it can ferment in the large bowel and cause loose, watery motions. Tofu (bean curd) protein can be given in reasonable quantities to increase protein content and quality. One of the main difficulties is to make such products flavoursome without the addition of some animal protein. Rice, pasta, soya and tofu can all be fried in olive oil which adds fat and flavour. Nut meat, which is protein derived from vegetable matter, will also assist in elevating the protein content of the diet and may increase the palatability of the diet.

A dog can be maintained on the most meagre of diets. Adult dogs can do well on half-rations but growing puppies can suffer severe problems of the bony skeleton if the diet is not balanced. Equating it to human terms, the growth rate from puppyhood to adulthood in a dog is completed in nine to twelve months. In a human growth phase, it is eighteen to twenty-one years. The rapid growth of dogs means that any shortcomings in the diet during this period are quickly felt in their metabolism. A diet that is insufficient in calcium will see the bones greatly thinned out and even fracture without any abnormal stresses. It is vital that if you elect to place your puppy on a vegetarian diet, you discuss it fully with a nutritional expert such as your vet. To subject a dog to a diet that will eventually cause it harm is a form of cruelty. Take time to understand what essential minerals and vitamins are needed to maintain reasonable growth rates and proper development of the skeleton.

Studies have shown that dogs need essential oils such as Omega 3 or high quality polyunsaturated oils to maintain good quality of skin and coat. Recent nutritional trials have also revealed that dogs do well on a high level of protein, around 30 per cent, so your dog's diet needs to be closely scrutinised if you are going to give it more than just a basic maintenance meal. Serious calculations should be made. And providing the dog accepts the food readily and maintains good condition without any signs of continuous illness, its diet is probably satisfactory. Weigh your dog monthly and talk to your vet about what would be considered a reasonable weight. Combine this with a good exercise program and a dog can live on a vegetarian diet, providing you are prepared to fulfil all of the minimum nutritional requirements.

31. Do dogs get food allergies?

The number of dogs that really have a food allergy is fewer than the number of dogs diagnosed with the condition. Far too often, if a dog has a non-seasonal propensity to scratch it is diagnosed as having a food allergy without proper testing.

To determine if a dog is allergic to particular food products, an elimination diet is essential. A reasonable elimination diet is cooked rice and lamb — this needs to be fed exclusively with no additives and without tasty snacking between meals. Nothing else in the environment needs to be changed. In the case of a true food allergy, improvement will be seen after seven days with the dog's skin looking normal by the end of three weeks.

Although food allergies are uncommon, often dogs with allergic skin disease appear to derive benefits from hypo-allergenic diets, or diets that are free from chemical preservatives. More and more manufacturers of commercial dog foods have moved away from using chemicals to preserve food using natural anti-oxidants such as vitamin E.

If your dog does improve on an elimination diet, it could be useful to include additives such as polyunsaturated oils, omega oils and other natural oils found in various herbs. The critical thing is to add only one additive at a time. The best starting point is omega oils: add this at the recommended dose for at least six weeks. If there is no deterioration in symptoms then another additive can be given. If the lamb and rice diet has been working, the next additive should be in the form of raw bone. These must be of sheep (ovine) origin, so use mutton flaps, lamb necks or brisket bones from sheep. Again, no other additive should be given for another six weeks.

The basis of the diet could become a good quality super-premium dry food as long as the preservatives, additives and basic ingredients are similar to those settled upon during the elimination diet. Lamb, rice, vitamin E, even omega oils or other polyunsaturated oils are all common ingredients found in the more superior prepared foods.

32. When do female puppies first come into season?

The scientific answer is that bitches come into their first season or cycle when they reach 75 per cent of their mature body weight.

In practical terms, toys and many terriers such as Maltese, Jack Russells, Cavalier King Charles spaniels and pugs usually have their first season (oestrus) around six months of age. The range for small dogs to have the first oestrus is six to nine months. Larger breeds have a range from nine to eighteen months, although it is not abnormal for some giant breeds to have their first cycle at two years of age.

33. At what age should I de-sex my dog?

Many animal welfare organisations endeavour to de-sex all dogs as early as possible in the effort to prevent these animals producing more unwanted pets. Physiologically this is not always best for the animal.

You do need to think about a few problems associated with early de-sexing of bitches. Bones are the first consideration. In humans it is recognised that lack of oestrogen leads to osteoporosis and some specialists feel that dogs that are de-sexed early have some decrease in bone mass.

The vulva and vagina are obviously under hormonal influence. Without hormones from a cycle, this area remains immature leading to problems such as infantile dermatitis or early urinary incontinence. While both of these conditions can be treated with hormone replacement therapy, prevention remains simpler than cure. Allowing a bitch to have one or two cycles, providing she can be locked away safely from any stray male, can be of benefit to the individual.

In males, de-sexing can take one of two forms. The most common is removal of the testicles. However, some people prefer to render the dog infertile by vasectomy. The first method has the advantage of calming down an over-enthusiastic dog. It most definitely helps to take aggression out of dogs and, if performed early enough, will stop sexual behaviour, which can be undesirable in a household with young children.

Males have the same consideration with age of de-sexing. Performed early, the dog doesn't have time to physically develop. Some vets say that de-sexing causes some breeds to broaden and deepen so much it can increase their propensity to bloat.

By the same token, allowed to remain entire, a male dog can

develop a desire to roam in search of females and can become aggressive. Castration is always recommended in dogs that take on aggressive behaviour, but if done too late it may not be of benefit.

Analyse this to work out when to de-sex your dog:

1 Can I, with every confidence, train my dog not to be aggressive?
2 Are my fences totally secure so that dogs can neither jump nor dig into or out of my backyard?
3 Does my dog live in a situation where I can definitely ensure that no mating will occur?
4 Do I own two dogs, a male and female, both entire?
5 Is the breed I have selected definitely not prone to being aggressive?
6 Is my dog gentle with my children, never displaying overt sexual behaviour?

No to any of these questions means that you should consider early de-sexing for your dog.

34. What do I do when two dogs are stuck together?

Owners become very concerned about this situation but dogs have been mating like this for centuries. The main thing is to not stress them because if they try to run or you try to separate them forcibly, harm can come to both of them. The bitch could tear and the male can end up with a fractured penis. The male canine is one of only two species that actually has a bone in the penis.

35. Can dogs get venereal disease?

While there are some cases of venereal disease in dogs, they are relatively uncommon. A slight yellow discharge at the tip of the dog's prepuce or sheath is often seen in mature dogs and is of little clinical consequence. Male dogs commonly have inflammation of the prepuce and this is referred to in veterinary terms as balanoposthitis. The amount of discharge can vary depending upon the degree of inflammation or alternatively the degree of sexual stimulation the dog receives. For example, a male dog that lives with a female dog may produce more discharge simply because of heightened sexual awareness and therefore more glandular activity. This is not a form of venereal disease and most cases resolve without therapy.

If the discharge appears excessive, then veterinary intervention may be required. The first stage of treatment can be attempted at home by douching the region with a dilute antiseptic such as chlorhexidine. This should not be used on breeding animals as it can lead to infertility. In breeding animals, a sterile saline solution may suffice to cleanse the area, although some reproductive experts suggest a light douche with diluted iodine and saline mixed together. In persistent cases, your vet would prescribe an antibiotic ointment, which needs to be placed gently into the prepuce, as well as administering broad spectrum oral antibiotics for seven to ten days.

Recurrence of mild infection of the prepuce is not uncommon despite therapeutic measures. In such cases de-sexing may prove useful to prevent any long-term problems with infection of the area.

An uncommon venereal disease in dogs is a transmissible canine venereal tumour. This presents as a cauliflower-like growth often seen growing deep in the prepuce and, in females, inside the vagina. The most common presenting sign is bleeding from the penis or the vulva as the tumour is often inflamed and is ulcerating. To diagnose this correctly, the dog would require a general anaesthetic so that inspection up inside the vagina or within the prepuce can be properly effected.

Metastasis (the ability of a tumour to break off and flow through the body and then grow elsewhere such as the lungs or the liver) is relatively uncommon in transmissible venereal tumours of dogs. However, the fact that they ulcerate causing bleeding and infection means that treatment must be instigated. This is one tumour where chemotherapy has proven extremely successful.

A bacterial venereal disease does occur but quarantine laws have seen it contained in America and certain parts of Europe.

The majority of breeds throughout the world require their bitches to have bacterial cultures taken from the vagina once they commence their season, prior to the actual mating period. The majority of workers in the field of canine reproduction dispute the need for this practice, stating that the majority of bacteria are normal flora within the female canine reproductive tract. They state that vaginal swabs are only necessary when a bitch shows signs of bacterial infection. The problems arise when owners fail to observe the sign of a vaginal infection, especially if a bitch tends to keep herself scrupulously clean by licking the region. If you are uncertain about the likelihood of a vaginal infection and you are about to breed your bitch, it may be wise to err on the side of caution and have a culture properly performed by a trained vet.

36. How can we ensure that we have a trouble-free litter?

Entire books have been written about breeding and whelping bitches, so we'll just cover the basic points here to assist you in whelping your first litter. There are a few decisions that need to be considered prior to embarking on breeding your animal.

Firstly, can you find good homes for the puppies?

Secondly, is your bitch actually worth breeding from? That is to say, while you love her dearly, does your animal carry any inheritable problems that may be inherited in the puppies? Temperament is the most important consideration, so if your bitch is antisocial, aggressive or hyper-excitable, think carefully before breeding from her. Are there any physical, heritable defects that your female carries? A veterinary examination will discover if there are problems that should not be promoted into the next generation. It is your responsibility to ensure that these puppies are given every chance of being both mentally and physically sound.

The male you choose to be the father (sire) of the puppies should also be well scrutinised for temperament and physical soundness. Your vet may recommend screening tests for your bitch, it is reasonable to expect the potential sire to have also undertaken similar testing procedures. Ensure that you sight proper certification with results that pass the male animal for breeding and keep a copy to show potential puppy buyers that you have undertaken to breed sound animals.

Any female undergoing a pregnancy must be in the prime of good health. Her vaccination program must be up to date and worming regime thorough. Prior to breeding, your bitch should not be too fat and her muscle development should be maximised by an enjoyable walking program, and this should continue throughout the pregnancy.

A bitch should not be bred from on her first cycle as most domestic dogs are too physically and mentally immature during the first oestrus. Generally, the third or fourth cycle is the optimum time to mate your bitch. By then you should have noticed how often she comes into cycle; that is, the length of time from one oestrus period to the next. This is very useful information as you need to be vigilant about the first day of her oestrus cycle.

Once your bitch starts the cycle on which you have chosen to have her mated, you need to count from the first day that you sight blood discharging from the vulva. On average the bitch will enter her fertile period — that is the time in which you must mate her — some 10 to 14 days after bleeding commences. This is an average, so you may elect to actually pinpoint her fertile period through blood tests. Your vet can take a sample looking for a progesterone rise and can then interpret exactly when she should be mated. This maximises the chance of conception as well as ensuring you get a good-sized litter.

You should be present at the mating in an endeavour to ensure your bitch has no problems in accepting what is happening. Three weeks after mating has occurred, you should make an appointment with your vet for an ultrasound to determine whether or not she is pregnant and to estimate of the size of the litter your bitch is expecting. Should your bitch have only conceived one or two puppies, it is very likely there may not be sufficient pressure on her cervix to instigate normal birth.

In canines, the normal gestation period, that is the time from mating to whelping, is 63 days.

Once the bitch enters her last trimester, six weeks after mating, she should be introduced into the area that has been prepared for her to deliver her puppies. This should be free from draughts, easy to warm or cool and not in a traffic zone. Continuous interruption through loud noises or visitations by unwanted people can make a bitch suppress the release of oxytocin, which actually generates contraction of the uterus. The bottom line is that the wrong environment places the puppies and the bitch at risk.

Given a good whelping area, the bitch will usually commence nesting during the final week leading up to the birth of the puppies. In the last 48 hours, the hormone called relaxin is secreted in her body in large doses. This softens the ligaments of the pelvis, thus opening the birth canal. All the ligaments become slacker and the bitch is said to drop in the flanks; this is seen as a hollowing out of the area just in front of the pelvis and below the loin region. The bitch takes on a somewhat Jersey cow type appearance in the back end giving us a sign that she will whelp shortly. When the hormone progesterone stops being produced to maintain the pregnancy, the bitch's body temperature drops for a short period. If the owner is monitoring her body temperature, usually morning and night, a drop to around 37°C is an indication that she will enter labour within 24 hours.

The nesting continues throughout this period with the bitch tearing up newspaper or scratching at whatever bedding has been provided. As the cervix starts to contract, the foetal fluids are released and the bitch enters the next stage of labour. The first puppy can be expected within one to two hours with further pups being delivered, on average, every hour. Providing the bitch is in the correct environment, there is usually little need for human intervention other than observing and monitoring.

If the bitch is continually straining and failing to produce a puppy within 40 minutes of serious muscular contractions it is time to seek veterinary assistance. This may indicate a bad presentation and a puppy stuck in the birth canal. You should also seek the help of a professional if the bitch fails to deliver a puppy every hour or so. For any one of many reasons a bitch can enter uterine inertia, the state in which the bitch lies with puppies in the uterus but fails to push and expel them. Your vet will be the best person to decide what type of medical or surgical interference is required. It is important that you have established a relationship with a reliable veterinary practice that provides a 24-hour service, as many whelpings occur in the middle of the night.

Unlike many species, the bitch cannot afford to go overtime from the expected date — once 48 hours has passed from the day you expect the puppies then it is time to seek veterinary advice.

When your bitch has finished whelping, she will settle quietly to feed her puppies. Puppies are born without protection against infections and require the mother's first milk to absorb antibodies (proteins that fight infections) into their own bloodstream. If you have developed a good relationship with your bitch, she will allow you occasionally to handle the puppies. Each day you should record the weights of your puppies. If any individual is not putting on weight then you should seek professional help. The exception to this is the first 24 hours of life where a puppy will often lose a small portion of its body weight.

You will need to know the body weights of the puppies from two weeks of age as worming preparations are administered at this time. In the majority of cases, puppies that are wormed at two weeks, four weeks and six weeks of age will not run into difficulties. If, after a worming preparation has been given, you see adult worms in the droppings, it may be necessary to worm more frequently.

Weaning of your puppies will commence around three or four weeks of age depending upon their development, breed, number of puppies, condition and the condition of your bitch. Do not offer the puppies cows' milk or cereal to commence the weaning process — this usually leads to diarrhoea (scouring) as they may not be able to competently digest the sugars in the milk. In the wild, pups receive regurgitated food from the mother to start their weaning process. For domestic dogs, a super-premium dry food, soaked in warm water to ensure it fully softens, is often a good starting point.

Once the puppies have accepted the new food and eagerly await their meals, it is time to remove the bitch from the puppies. This should be done over a period of about one week, continually increasing the time the bitch spends away from the puppies. It is important to know that the more time the bitch spends time away from the puppies the more she will continue to produce milk. If her milk is not drying up then you may need to seek professional help so that drugs can be administered to suppress further lactation.

At six weeks your puppies will need to be taken to your vet for vaccinations. During this time your vet will examine them for any obvious congenital or heritable problems, especially things like heart defects, obvious eye problems or kneecaps that may go in and out of joint. It is impossible to tell whether a puppy will develop things like hip dysplasia, hereditary elbow problems or so many other conditions that can only be detected later on in life. However, as a breeder you may well be responsible for these conditions so you need to consider what form of guarantee you are going to offer your buyers. If commonsense prevails you will offer a full refund should the puppy develop a debilitating heritable defect in the first two years of life.

After vaccination you should keep the puppies for two weeks, allowing them to take up the vaccine, and ensuring there is no adverse reaction. With the sale of each puppy, provide a diet sheet, a sample of the food they have been eating and some of the water from your taps that the puppies are used to drinking.

It all sounds like a lot of work and it is, but if you do it properly breeding dogs can be a very satisfying experience.

37. How do I stop my dog from farting all the time?

There are several possibilities that lead to increased gas production in a dog's intestine. Regardless of the cause, the end result appears the same — your dog can clear a crowded room in seconds. Trying to pinpoint the reason and control the problem meets with varying results.

Soya meal, which is used in many dog foods both wet and dry, increases both hydrogen and carbon dioxide in a dog's bowel. Diets that are high in fibre and contain fermentable sugars as carbohydrate will also produce large volumes of gas.

Other causes of flatulence can arise from conditions that cause poor digestion, leaving nutrients in the gut that will ferment and produce gas. Malabsorption, maldigestion and pancreatic insufficiency are typical of the problems that may be associated with flatulence. Gas production can also be as a result of aerophagia, swallowing of air.

There are several things you can do to solve this problem. Try a high quality, easily digested dog food. One of the super-premium dry food products would be your best starting point. Avoid foods that are high in soya meal, milk, sugars or fats and fibre. In addition, as a general rule, canned food is out. Some of the refrigerated meat loafs appear to be of benefit and they can be mixed with super-premium dry food.

Additives that can assist are such things as charcoal tablets to absorb excess toxins from the gut, carminatives such as dill, ginger or peppermint to remove excess swallowed gas or enzymes that aid digestion especially in cases of poor digestion.

38. What can I do when my dog is constipated?

Constipation is defined as the absence of or infrequent bowel movements to evacuate the colon. What home remedy you may wish to instigate will depend upon how much pain the dog is displaying and how often it is managing to pass faeces, both of which are directly bound to the cause of constipation. If the dog is continually straining, crying out in pain, then it is time to seek urgent veterinary assistance.

Cases of constipation can be so severe that the build up of toxins and/or splitting of the intestines inside the body can lead to death of the animal. Tenesmus, continual but ineffectual straining to defecate, can result in a condition called megacolon. This is an extremely enlarged bowel that can no longer push faeces out of the rectum.

If your dog is passing hard, dry faeces with obvious difficulty then some home remedies may be attempted. Firstly, examine the diet. It should contain sufficient fibre or bulk in the form of vegetable matter. The dog should also have ready access to water and you should ensure that the dog has been drinking sufficient quantities. Oil should be immediately added to the diet in the form of either paraffin straight into the mouth and swallowed, or vegetable oil mixed into the food. Cooked vegetables should also be added to the diet, especially those containing much fibre and fluid such as marrow, squash, cabbage, carrot and zucchini. The dog might only eat these mixed with a little minced meat and or gravy. A little extra salt sprinkled over the food will encourage an increase in water consumption.

With dogs that regularly become constipated the diet may need to be examined for an excess of bones. Cooked bones especially lead to constipation as the cooking process collapses the matrix of the bone rendering it indigestible to the dog's gastric juices.

If, despite reasonable efforts, your dog continues to become constipated then there may be an underlying cause. One of the most common causes of constipation in mature to aged male dogs is blockage of the pelvic outlet by an enlarged prostate. Your vet will need to perform either a digital examination of the rectum or ultrasonography of the region in order to establish the size of the prostate. If this gland is proven to be enlarged then therapy for prostatitis will need to be instigated, either in the form of female hormones or the more permanent resolution by castration.

Old dogs can develop what is called a neurogenic colon. This is where abnormalities of the spine (usually degeneration of the bony spinal column causing severe osteoarthritis) results in the deterioration of good nerve supply to the large bowel.

This causes a decrease in the muscle tone of the large bowel as well as decreasing the ability of the nervous system to send a message to the brain, reminding the animal it is time to defecate. Faecal softeners and bulking agents are usually not sufficient to reverse this problem. Often the animal will require an anaesthetic and evacuation of the large bowel by an enema or even surgical intervention. If the dog has already developed a megacolon the long term prognosis is very bad. A vet will need to instigate drug therapy in an endeavour to re-establish reasonable colonic function. However, this is not always possible.

In younger dogs with chronic constipation, where the diet is found to be adequate other causes need to be identified. Fractures of the pelvis that may have occurred much earlier in life could easily lead to obstruction of the pelvic outlet. Tumours, even benign masses, can occur in the region and are also capable of blocking normal bowel function. For these reasons, as well as other possible causes, it is important to seek professional help if constipation continues to pose a problem despite owners making reasonable efforts with diet and laxatives. The condition is often underestimated and many cases are presented too late to save the dog's life.

39. My dog has just passed a watery bowel movement. Do I need to go to the vet?

Loose bowel motions or diarrhoea is the most common complaint to vets by dog owners. This possibly reflects the behaviour of dogs to eat what humans would regard as rather undesirable material. Also many owners take the attitude with their own food that if it is 'off', feed it to the dog. Consequently, a single bout of loose motions probably does not signify the need to seek veterinary assistance.

If a dog has one or two loose bowel movements then home therapy should include fasting for twenty-four hours. If you can't bring yourself to not feed your dog, then at least provide very bland food in the form of cooked rice mixed with a little well-cooked chicken or cooked mince. Home remedies may also be administered in the form of activated charcoal. Activated charcoal may not be readily available but other products might be easier to access such as kaolin or pectin, both found in many off-the-shelf human anti-diarrhoeals. Even if there is no access to such items you might find something useful in your own kitchen. Gelatine or cornflower can both be administered in an endeavour to place a lining on the inside of the bowel and firm the faeces.

If the diarrhoea persists or should there be copious amounts of blood then professional assistance must be sought. Blood indicates a severe cause as the internal lining of the bowel has been sufficiently attacked to strip the mucous layer thereby exposing the more delicate layer containing blood vessels. Your vet will test for infectious agents and may need to endoscope your dog for the possibility of ulcers in the colon (ulcerative colitis) or take a sample to detect the presence of bowel cancer.

Parasites are a very common reason for diarrhoea, so check your worming program. Also have a faecal test performed at your local veterinary clinic. This will not only ensure that your choice of worming product is effective but it will also rule out the possibility of protozoa which can inflame the bowel, leading to chronic watery motions.

Food allergies are often considered as a cause of chronic diarrhoea but in truth they are very rare in dogs. Nevertheless, some simple testing might find a product that disagrees with your dog. Try a bland diet of just two products and if this appears to control the dog's diarrhoea then only one type of food should be added on a weekly basis. Cooked rice and either cooked skinless chicken or cooked lean mutton or lamb is often a good starting point as it avoids the possibilities of a wheat allergy or the histamine release that is sometimes seen when beef is fed. Should this initially work then after two weeks cooked potato or pumpkin could be added to the diet. The process continues, adding a different product each fortnight until a balanced diet that does not cause diarrhoea is finally developed for the animal.

40. How can I stop my dog eating its own poo?

Coprophagia, or eating of faeces, is not uncommon in dogs and can even be considered natural. Regardless of how natural it may be, the habit is extremely distasteful for humans to watch and it becomes even more disgusting when an animal that has just eaten poo gives you a big lick across the face!

Treating a dog that exhibits coprophagic behaviour can be quite difficult. Parasites (worms and other bugs) can be one cause of coprophagia. Lack of a balanced diet, insufficient vitamins (especially B-group), inability to produce enough enzymes to digest food, or low minerals in the diet are other reasons dogs eat their own poo or that of others.

Check that the dog is on a good quality balanced diet, which includes some mineral and vitamin supplements. Raw bones, two or three times each week are useful in this endeavour.

Monthly worming is recommended for dogs that eat their own droppings and a faecal test can show if there are any unusual parasites. Tapeworm can pose an unusual problem, and as it doesn't readily appear in faecal tests you need to assume your dog has it and administer medication specific for this family of worms. If you live in an area where frogs are common or if you feed your dog fish, you should give a double dose of tapeworm medication as your pet could harbour spirometra (zipper tapeworm), a very long tapeworm whose cysts are found in frogs and fish.

Your vet can perform a blood test to see if your dog has pancreatic insufficiency and does not produce sufficient enzymes to digest food properly. If the test result is on the lower side of normal you should consider using pancreatic enzyme supplements. Alternatively, you might consider just adding some enzymes to the diet to see if there is an improvement in the coprophagic behaviour.

Sometimes you can do all these things — worm your dog, give a dietary supplement, add enzymes, improve the diet — and still the problem persists.

So what now? Well, either a habit has formed that needs to be broken or it's natural and your dog is simply recycling any proteins that were missed or adding B-group vitamins, commonly found in faecal material, to its diet.

You may need to think about negative reinforcement. Smothering droppings with Tabasco sauce has often been used to discourage this behaviour, but don't be surprised if it simply causes your dog to develop a liking for the sauce. Red cayenne pepper in powder form can replace the sauce; as the dog sniffs the droppings, the smell will repel your dog's gastronomic intentions.

If you can find them, some human deodorant tablets (they're taken orally to reduce body odour) or the tablets used to minimise smells in bitches in season (chlorophyll tablets) can be given to make the faeces taste terrible. If these tablets are not available, you might want to discuss with your vet the option of some herbal or other oral preparation that could help make the poo taste terrible.

Some training may be required. Always use the same word and tone when you are chastising your dog. Whatever word you utilise, make sure you 'growl' the word out. This is exactly the manner utilised by the dog's mother to a pup or pack leader to an adult. The growl is an important method of well-understood communication in the canine world. The word no is commonly used as the human vocal chords can wrap themselves into a growl when enunciating the word. You should utilise this negative reinforcement when your dog even sniffs faecal material.

Another method is to use a hose and spray the dog when it approaches faecal material in the yard. It is important that you hide yourself and your dog does not realise that you are present and the cause of the nasty jet of water. The dog soon associates the intention to ingest faeces with a very negative experience.

Finally, if all else fails, leave lots of raw bones and toys lying around the yard to entertain the dog, and clean up any poo quickly.

41. How does trouble with the prostate gland affect dogs?

Old male dogs, just like old male humans, will often have problems with their prostate. Because we do not notice the volume of urinary flow in our dogs, the symptoms presented to the vet are the more severe ones, such as blood in the urine or constipation. The prostate enlarges because of cysts forming within it. The condition is referred to as cystic hyperplasia and can vary in severity from a few large cysts to multiple large numbers of small cysts. In both cases the cysts are formed as a result of the effect of testosterone on the prostate. The male hormone testosterone promotes secretion of fluid by the prostate and this continuous action results often in cyst formation.

Not as common is the formation of an actual abscess within the prostate. Although the prostate becomes very inflamed, it does not always develop a secondary bacterial infection. This is why anti-biotics alone will probably do little to assist in the treatment of prostatitis. The inflammation, as well as the cysts themselves, destroys much of the normal architecture of the prostate, causing severe decrease in the integrity of the blood vessels within the gland, thus resulting in the haemorrhage that is often associated with this disease. Male dogs that become sexually aroused and have an enlarged prostate can develop an acute bout of prostatitis because of the testosterone rush.

Therapy for prostatitis varies greatly depending upon the severity of the case and the owner's desire to keep the testicles on the dog. Ideally the prostate fluid should be sent for culture to diagnose whether a secondary bacterial infection has occurred and allow the appropriate antibiotic to be used. If the dog is to be bred from, then one of two alternatives is possible. A Swedish study has found posi-tive results in minimising the problem through the use of a female hormone. This is given as a course of injections over a period of six to twelve weeks. The dog's sperm count will usually diminish during therapy, but given sufficient time most males return to reasonable levels of fertility. The other alternative is a daily tablet called finastride, which has been extremely successful in the treatment of human prostatitis. This therapy is reasonably expensive and you need to consider how long you can afford to keep your dog on this type of medication.

A permanent cure for prostatitis is castration. In fact, all dogs with severe prostatitis should at some stage face this surgical procedure as it once and for all removes any pain and inflammation from the prostate. Continuing medical therapy can only control prostatitis for a limited period of time. Removing the prostate surgically renders the dog infertile and is a far more intrusive and severe surgical procedure than castration. Therefore, the most valuable of stud dogs, if truly loved and appreciated by his owner, would one day face castration if he developed prostatitis.

42. How can my dog get a stone in its bladder?

Bladder stones form because compounds in the urine encourage the formation of crystals. Diet and infection are the usual reasons these compounds are found in the bladder; the compounds build crystals and combine with mucus, forming larger stones. As the stones grow in size, they erode and irritate the inside of the bladder. Consequently, the dog develops bloody urine and continually strains to urinate. If the bladder becomes totally blocked the dog may cry out in pain.

Diagnosis is usually made by your vet through an X-ray. Most stones can easily be seen on a radiograph. However, one type of stone (urate crystal), common in Dalmatians, fails to show up. In such cases, ultrasound or special contrast media used with X-rays is required to make a correct diagnosis.

Bladder stones will usually need to be surgically removed. Some types may respond to special diet and flushing, but this depends upon the individual case, so take your vet's advice. The degree of difficulty in the surgery depends upon the location of all the stones. Those found in the bladder are easily removed by opening the dog's abdomen (a laparotomy). However, stones trapped in the tube going from the bladder to the penis or vulva (the urethra) can be difficult to clear. Sometimes it can be effected by simple catheterisation but other times a cutting down to and opening the tube itself (a ure-throstomy) is necessary.

Once your dog's urinary tract is cleared of stones, special dietary requirements must be followed in an attempt to stop re-occurrence of bladder stones. The diet will largely depend upon the type of stone recovered from your dog's bladder. These will be sent to a laboratory for analysis and your vet can then recommend the necessary dietary changes. Each stone will develop under varying acidity of the urine or may be enhanced by certain dietary components. The pH of the urine can be adjusted with such products as vitamin C, ammonium chloride or even apple cider vinegar. In addition, there is a plethora of commercial foods registered to assist in the dietary control of urinary tract problems. Your vet will have a favourite food so talk to them as to what best suits your dog's condition.

Sometimes, commercial foods for urinary tract problems can be unpalatable or expensive. Your vet can research some home recipes that might be more inviting for your dog to eat and far less expensive on your pocket.

Australian shepherd (see page 6)

Bichon Frise (see page 7)

Boxer (see page 8)

Cavalier King Charles spaniel (see page 9)

German shepherd (see page 10)

Golden retriever (see page 12)

Hungarian Vizsla puppy

Hungarian Vizsla (see page 13)

Labrador retriever puppy

Labrador retriever (see page 14)

Pekingese (see page 15)

Poodles (see page 16)

Pug (see page 17)

Dr Rob Zammit on his property at Vineyard, NSW,
with seven of his twelve dogs.

43. What should I do about worming my dog?

Worms are parasites that not only affect dogs but can also affect humans. To avoid an out-of-control situation with worms, follow these rules:

- Worm your dog regularly. Once per month if they are always walking where there are other dogs or, at least, once every three months if they don't often associate with other dogs.
- Always pick up dog droppings as soon as possible, keeping your yard and the environment free of contamination, not just from faecal material but also from worm eggs.
- Teach children to always wash their hands after playing with the dog and ensure that you do the same.
- Never feed your dog offal (liver, kidneys, heart etc) as these can contain larvae from a seriously nasty tapeworm called hydatid worms.

To appreciate why you need to worm so frequently let's examine the worm's life cycle.

Worm eggs hatch in the environment, especially in warm, moist conditions. Dogs then pick up these hatchlings, called larvae, when they sniff or lick an infected area.

The larvae are swallowed and enter the intestinal tract. The larvae then burrow through into the bloodstream of the dog. From there, the larvae migrate through the body moving into the lungs, where they eventually mature. Finally, they are coughed up the windpipe, swallowed, then they re-enter the intestinal tract as adult worms which eventually lay their own eggs. The whole process for round-worms and hookworms takes three weeks.

The problem is that when you worm your dog, you can only kill the adult worms in the intestinal tract at the time the medication is going through. Twenty-four hours after dosing, a dog can have worms again if they have lots of larvae throughout their lungs. The immature larvae are not affected by any medication.

The scenario is even more complicated with puppies because they can pick up worm larvae while in their mother's uterus as well as while suckling from her. Combine that with an immature immune system and it's little wonder that pups can be infected with worms from seven days of age onwards! Therefore it is essential that breeders worm their pups early in life and that owners continue an intensive worming regime.

Heartworm

One of the nasty critters in the world of worms is the heartworm. As the name implies this worm lives inside a dog's heart. Mosquitoes are the intermediate host for these worms. If an unprotected canine is bitten by a mosquito carrying a heartworm larvae, the dog will develop heartworm within six months.

Heartworms live in the pulmonary arteries and right atrium of the heart, eventually causing congestive heart failure concluding in the death of the host. Infected dogs can be treated with arsenic but obviously prevention is far better than cure. There are many medications that are easily available to prevent this dreadful disease but one, milbemycin, also treats hook, round and whipworm so it would seem the logical choice. It's available as a once-a-month tablet, so you are regularly dosing for most intestinal parasites while keeping your dog protected from heartworm.

An annual injection for heartworm is available and the timing of this injection can be combined with other vaccinations, meaning that one trip to the vet each year helps keep your dog healthy and free of these dreadful parasites. You need to remember that intestinal parasites will still be a problem so worming at least four times each year will be essential.

Tapeworm

The other type of worm you need to consider is tapeworm. Broadly, the main types that need to be treated are the common flea tapeworm and the hydatid tapeworm. The problem of flea tapeworm is easily addressed by controlling fleas and routine worming with tapeworm products, especially after a flea infestation. Hydatid tapeworm is more serious, but it can be prevented.

In New Zealand, because of the large risk to human health by hydatid, an eradication program has been in existence for many years and recently Tasmania has embarked on a similar program. Each year, new cases of hydatid cysts are found in Australians, which is a poor indictment on community health concerns in this country. While it's mainly seen in the country areas, because sheep are the principal intermediate host, it can occur in anyone who allows their dog to eat offal (liver, intestines, kidneys and other organs). Offal can harbour hydatid cysts and is the only way a dog can become infected. Because dogs in country areas may eat these tissues without their owners realising, it is essential to worm dogs, especially in high-risk regions, every six weeks. Although these two initiatives seem simple enough, they are yet to be instigated to exterminate this problem which is not an uncommon human health risk.

The third variety is sometimes called 'zipper' tapeworm because of obvious segmentation and a marked dark region down its centre-line. The worm causes some gut pain in severely infected dogs due to mechanical interference with intestinal movement because of the sheer length of these worms. Frogs are the intermediate host for the 'zipper' tapeworm, which is technically called spirometra. The problem is that spirometra is a stubborn worm usually needing two to three times the dose of tapeworm medication to get rid of the horrid thing.

Some people think that their children are safe from worms transmitted by dogs as long as they worm their children regularly, but this is wrong. In children, worm larvae that have been picked up from dogs do not mature as adult worms in the child's intestine and are not affected by any worm medicine you administer. The larvae can have devastating effects on children, so it is vital that you follow a strict worming regime for your dog.

If you have children at home then when you introduce a new puppy to the household it is best to assume it has worms. Pups should be wormed on the first day they arrive into your home. Repeat the worming weekly for the next two weeks then commence using a monthly heartworm tablet that also covers intestinal parasites. If you add tapeworm therapy at the commencement of every season you will essentially never have trouble with worms in your dog.

Ringworm

Ringworm is fungal skin infection and people commonly make the error of thinking this condition is some kind of parasite, like roundworm or threadworm. For more information on ringworm, see pages 151.

Analyse this to work out whether you have adequate worm control :

1 Is your dog on regular preventative medication for heartworm?
2 Do you administer a worming preparation for hook, round and whipworm at least four times per year?
3 Do you have adequate flea control for your dog?
4 Is a tapeworm medication given each spring, summer, autumn and winter?
5 Are you certain that your dog never has access to offal?
6 Are the droppings from the dog immediately removed from your yard?
7 Do you and your children wash their hands after playing with the dog?

If you answer no to any of the first five questions then you probably do not have adequate worm control for your dog.

Answer no to any of the last three questions, then you are putting your family at a risk of being infected with worm larvae.

44. My dog keeps rubbing his bottom along the ground. Is it worms?

When dogs place their bottom on the ground and drag it along the grass, it is called 'scooting'. This happens whenever a dog gets an itchy or inflamed anal region. While worms can be one cause of such a problem, a more common cause for scooting is anal glands impaction.

The anal glands are two secretory sacs located at the four o'clock and eight o'clock position around the anus. They fill with a dark, foul-smelling, thick substance that is released when a dog is frightened. Some of the fluid is also released if a dog is passing very dry, hard faecal material as the anal secretions are fatty, therefore lubricating the region.

The anal glands or sacs are connected by means of very small ducts (or canals). These can easily become blocked, especially in smaller dogs, resulting in the sacs becoming impacted with the anal gland secretions. Unfortunately, infection will easily localise in this area, which is known for its colonisation by a varied range of bacterial flora. This further inflames the area and the dog tries to relieve itself by scooting and licking constantly under the tail. When this situation arises the only relief the dog can receive is by expressing the anal glands.

Using a gloved hand, your vet will squeeze each gland so that it forcibly unblocks the duct, emptying the contents of the anal sac. The process is painful so the owner needs to hold the front end of the dog firmly and a nurse might sometimes assist by holding the hindquarters still.

Professional dog groomers and some owners will learn the technique which is, in the most cases, relatively simple. At times it may require a more complicated approach, but the easiest way is to place a thumb just under one anal gland, index finger under the other then push in and squeeze together. If performed correctly, two things will happen. Firstly, the dog will have instant relief. Secondly, you will notice one of the foulest odours you have ever smelt emanating from the greasy fluid that is on the ground or on the gloved hand. Do it outside because you'll never get rid of the smell, especially if it oozes into carpet fibres.

Left unattended, without releasing the build-up of secretions, the pressure inside the sac will continue to rise, finally climaxing in a rupture of the skin to relieve the situation, like a pimple bursting. In fact, an anal abscess has been created which, unless professionally treated, will continue as a source of infection in the region. Dogs with an anal abscess soon go off their food, becoming listless as the toxins build up in their bloodstream, causing the dog to develop a fever and even vomit. This requires the poor animal to have surgical intervention, curetting the abscess and administering antibiotics.

If a dog requires the anal glands to be frequently released then surgical removal should be considered prior to severe abscessation of the region, which can lead to long-term problems. The whole region around the anus can become undermined with infection, which can take several attempts at surgery before it totally resolves.

45. Can you really get rid of fleas on a dog?

Ctenocephalides felis and the less common flea species *Ctenocephalides canis* are the most ubiquitous blood-sucking parasites that readily feed on dogs, cats and humans. They cause severe scratching with consequent allergic responses that are manifested in inflamed skin, loss of hair and often a moist dermatitis.

To understand about controlling fleas, you need to understand a little bit about the flea and its life cycle. Fleas can jump long distances and will attach themselves to animals like your dog that provide them with a meal. If you take your dog out for a walk and it picks up a dozen or so fleas, these will feed quite happily on your animal probably until they reach your home. At some stage the fleas will drop off your dog onto the animal's bedding, or your carpet, or they'll go under your house.

Only a dozen or so fleas have entered your house, but this is where the fun begins. Each female flea is capable of laying around 50 eggs each day of her life. And adult fleas themselves are fairly hardy. In a humid environment, fleas are known to be able to survive off their host for up to seven months without a blood meal. It is the feeding off the host that stimulates the females into laying eggs, and even if they lay them on your dog, the small white eggs do not adhere to the dog's skin or coat but roll off and infect the environment.

Given the right conditions of humidity, warmth, carbon dioxide levels and even vibrations, the eggs hatch and develop into larvae, quite happily living in the base of bedding or carpet. These larvae make a cocoon in which the larvae pupates, eventually hatching out as adult fleas. The time taken for an egg to complete its life cycle, forming into an egg-laying adult flea, is just three weeks. Think about this for a moment: a female flea comes into your house and three weeks later you have 50 more fleas. The next day, an extra 50 have hatched and now you have 100. Within a month of that flea having entered your house, you have 350 more fleas! You don't have to be a mathematician to realise that a month or so after a dozen fleas enter your house, you're in the middle of a flea plague.

So how can you effectively treat an ever-increasing army of blood-sucking parasites? Obviously you can't give family counselling to fleas, but you can stop them from reproducing. You do need to treat all animals in your household, dogs and cats, and be active in your chosen methods of therapy. Firstly, add lufenuron (Novartis) to your pet's food once a month. When fleas bite pets treated with this product, their eggs will fail to hatch. This stops the normal build-up that leads to the flea plague that is so commonly seen in households. Secondly, wash the animal's bedding regularly and vacuum your carpet thoroughly. Thirdly, use an effective but safe insecticide on all the pets in your household.

Our household has had very positive results from using lufenuron, which is a good sign, given that we live on five acres with some twelve or more dogs and half a dozen cats. We have not seen a flea plague on the property since we started using this product. The biggest headache is remembering to give it each month, and I find the first day of the month is the easiest way of remembering to dose the animals monthly.

It is important to realise that fleas harbour diseases. The bubonic plague was spread through fleas on rats, and fleas are actually the intermediate host of the common tapeworm of dogs. It is a good idea to worm them against tapeworm three to four weeks after a flea infection just to ensure that they do not become infected with an internal parasite.

46. Help! My dog is lost! What should I do?

If your dog is lost, chances are it will be drawn to places where other dogs live. Doorknock these houses and ask the owners if they have seen your dog — a picture of your pooch can be particularly useful in this endeavour. Continue widening the search area, covering a reasonable circle around your house.

The next step is to contact the local veterinary hospitals in the district. You should visit each one, introduce yourself to the receptionist, and leave a notice with a photograph. Ask the receptionist if they could make enquiries by pointing out your notice and asking clients if they've seen your dog.

Visit all the local council dog pounds and animal shelters and leave them a copy of your notice. Never simply rely on a telephone call to these centres as they have to deal with thousands of dogs and numerous calls each year. You could miss your dog while it's sitting on death row – this is a common occurrence, so visit during assigned times every couple of days, checking all the kennels for yourself.

Posters or notices placed on poles and walls, garages and market places can help but you may need to use the word 'reward' to encourage people's assistance. Pet recovery services are available and they do have connections that could prove useful. Their fees are usually reasonable so it's worth making an enquiry.

Everyone who owns a dog should ensure good identification. Microchipping is an obvious answer because it gives permanent identification to your dog, but microchips are only useful if they are registered on a national register. An identification collar is also useful, but as these can come adrift so they may not be permanent. Alternatively, you might have your telephone number tattooed in your dog's ear – this seems radical but it could save your dog's life. A smart idea is to take a photograph of your dog every six months so you have a recent identikit for your pooch. On the back of this, you should keep the dog's microchip or tattoo number.

Give your dog good environmental reasons not to leave home and ensure that gates and fences are secure for those dogs who feel that they simply must wander.

47. Do dogs require special care in summer?

In cooler areas where the summer temperatures are mild, generally nothing extra is required to maintain a dog's comfort. However, in areas of high humidity or where heat wave conditions result in very high temperatures, some special care is required. Aged canines are prone to collapse in the heat and extremely young animals, easily excited to a state where they overexercise during hot conditions, often suffer heat stress. Dogs that have trouble breathing, often those with squashed-in faces such as Pekingese, bulldogs or pugs, can find respiration even more distressing in very humid, hot conditions.

Shade for your dog is vital in the hot summer months. It is essential that there is a cool restful place with full shade throughout the day. Shadecloth placed over a wire run does not provide good enough shade in very hot conditions. Insulated kennels are ideal but these must be located in an area that has total shade during summer. The dog's water must be in a shaded area — warm or even hot water on a hot humid day is neither refreshing nor pleasant. The water bowl must not leak and it is a good idea to put out two water buckets in case one is accidentally tipped over. One of the water buckets could also contain the correct amount of electrolytes that assist in preventing dehydration. Some owners also place a container full of ice in a shaded area — this will remain cold for many hours and provide a cooling drink throughout the warmest part of the day.

White dogs or those with pale patches on the nose or tummy are prone to sunburn. For some reason, many of these dogs appear to enjoy sunbaking, commonly on their back exposing these pink areas to sunburn. The best answer is to enclose them in an area that is totally shaded throughout the day. If this is not possible, then a waterproof sunblock will reduce the possibilities of sunburn, which could develop into skin cancer.

Flies increase both in number and activity in summer and can become more than just a nuisance. They are capable of inflicting a bite on a dog's skin. The most common areas for bites are around the head, especially on the ear tips on prick-eared dogs and where the ears join the head on floppy-eared dogs, and the legs. The flies will eventually draw blood from these areas and, when the wounds are large enough, female flies will lay eggs that hatch into maggots causing flyblown skin on the dog.

Flytraps or flypaper can help in decreasing the number of flies and a good quality insect repellent applied to the dog can prevent flies from taking hold. The best fly repellents appear to be citronella-based, along with an extra insecticide. While dogs hate these being applied, often rubbing themselves on the grass after you apply it, the citronella oil remains on the skin and in the coat giving protection throughout the day.

Summertime is also a period when your worming program must be scrupulously followed. Mosquitoes increase their activity so heartworm infections can become more prevalent and intestinal worms hatch more frequently because of the moisture and warmth in the ground. Fleas are also more common and, as these are the intermediate hosts for the common tapeworm, flea treatment should also be current.

A bed that is well off the ground, allowing good ventilation underneath and properly positioned in a shaded or insulated area will improve your dog's comfort. A couple of freezer blocks placed under the bed each day can aid in the removal of heat stress.

Like people, dogs require fewer calories during the warmer months, so you need to observe your dog's weight carefully, as being fatter not only makes them uncomfortable but can make heat stress much more difficult to avoid. Always feed during the cool times in the day, either very early in the morning or late in the evening. The type of food can essentially remain the same; just give the dog less.

Probably the most exciting stimulant for a dog is the sight of strangers walking past the house, causing it run around and bark. In the case of young or excitable dogs a blind that blocks the line of sight to the outside world will assist in calming your dog and prevent it from overheating.

These initiatives take little effort and will make your dog more comfortable and healthy. If you own a breed that is not particularly suited to a hot environment, put some thought and forward planning into caring for your animal during summer.

48. What can I do when my dog gets too hot?

You need to make a clear distinction between a dog that is simply very warm because of high environmental temperatures and a dog that is truly heat-stressed.

Heatstroke (heat-stress or hyperpyrexia) is an emergency situation. Dogs become heat-stressed when confined in some overheated enclosure such as cars. Over-exercising in the heat of the day, locking dogs in pens with no shade or even leaving them in a trailer have all resulted in death from heat-stress.

The symptoms of heat-stress are collapse, hyperventilation and a very elevated body temperature. The gums may initially be maroon red, but as shock continues, gum colour changes to pale with a greyish tinge.

Treatment is initially aimed at getting the dog's body temperature down: ice packs, a cold bath and cool air-conditioned air will assist in this endeavour. Shock must be treated with intravenous fluids, high-potency intravenous cortisone to minimise brain swelling, a diuretic to try and stop kidney shutdown, and a bronchodilator to open airways and oxygen.

The dog could appear to return to normal but still die 24 hours later if 'malignant hyperthermia' has been reached. This is the critical body temperature that, once reached, will damage all the tiny blood vessels (capillaries) in the body. If this occurs, all the capillaries in the brain begin to rupture, and the dog will have seizures and usually die within a few hours.

49. What's the best bedding?

When you walk into any reasonable pet store there's always a section that seems like a bedding department, with everything from quilted rugs to waterbeds for dogs. One guy even tried to sell canine vibrating beds but, not surprisingly, they just didn't seem to take off!

The best bedding must offer the following comforts: cool in summer, warm in winter and easily cleaned to avoid the build-up of dirt, bacteria and flea eggs. To achieve these aims, the first consideration is that the bed must be raised off the ground. Beds that lie on concrete allow the cold straight through to your dog's bones — not much fun in the dark hours of a cold winter's night. An ideal location for dirt and fleas is directly underneath any bedding on the ground. Even if you have a proper wooden kennel, a raised bed helps a dog have a good night's sleep.

There are many ways you can raise a dog's bed off the ground. If you're looking for the cheapest method, then a wooden pallet or piece of plywood with a brick under each corner is a starting point. Up from that are various trampoline beds, the simplest of which is a metal frame made to fit a hessian sack. However, the sack will stretch and the thickness of the material does harbour dirt and other undesirables. A variation on this theme is made from PVC pipe and covered with shadecloth-like material, but dogs quickly manage to catch a tooth or nail in the material so it often shreds. The original trampoline-style bed, made with a metal frame and covered taut with canvas material is the most enduring and easiest to clean. You may pay more for the initial investment but, in my experience, it outlasts anything else by many years. A big plus is that it can be effectively hosed in the morning and it will be dry in a few hours, even on wet days.

During hot summer months, air circulating underneath the bed gives the best potential for a comfortable sleep, especially if the bed is strategically located under the house or inside an insulated kennel, which is itself under shade. During winter, an extra blanket can be thrown on top — the quilted variety will certainly be appreciated by your dog, in the same way that you enjoy that extra warmth in cold weather.

Bedsores, or callouses, do occur in old dogs if they sleep on hard surfaces, but are not seen on dogs that lie on trampoline beds. A layer of extra foam can help but in very young dogs this may end up inside the dog instead of under it!

50. What's the best lead and collar for my dog?

The collar that allows you to fully control your dog in the gentlest, kindest manner is the one you need.

Check chains have the potential to be misused so they become a choking device. A check chain must never be pulled tight and held firm around the dog's neck, otherwise they become 'choker' collars that could cause severe damage. Correct use of a check chain should allow the collar to be loose around the dog's neck for 99 per cent of the time. The lead is simply jerked lightly to gently influence the dog to respond to a specific command. The response must always finish with praise, as any exercise should be based on positive reinforcement and not chastisement, especially through abuse of the collar.

Halter-type collars are correctly based on an old adage, 'Control the head and you control the animal.' These very true words find proof in the fact that a small human can control a large horse, or even a bull, by the use of a halter or headstall. Most dogs do not accept being harnessed around the muzzle easily but food can be used as a distraction to help them embrace the idea a little more readily. Small morsels of some extra tasty bits of chicken or cooked liver can distract the dog from the irritating strap across the muzzle, while allowing the animal to understand that the function of its mouth is in no way hampered, providing, of course, that the dog follows your lead. The moment the dog attempts to pull ahead or tows you in a different direction, the harness tightens around the muzzle, lifting the dog's head and giving you control.

Soft collars simply allow an owner to walk a dog, but with little control. In fact, a dog can easily back out of a soft collar if it's not tight enough around the neck. Obedience schools that promote this method suggest that food be utilised as a reward, but this only works if you can convince the dog to do the right thing in the first place. On a long walk, you might find you've used the dog's daily ration just to keep the dog by your side!

In short, the best collar for your dog is the one that allows you full control in any situation without ever inflicting pain on your animal.

Leads are a different consideration again. In every case, the wrong lead is the steel chain. These can inflict pain across your hands if a dog pulls hard and they can become entangled around a dog's legs causing lacerations or even fractures.

The most effective lead is made of webbing material or leather and a length that you can use comfortably and efficiently. Leather leads are ideal for this situation, coming in all sorts of sizes and lengths. Webbing leads made from soft materials that are pliable yet very strong are popular at obedience schools, as they are relatively cheap.

51. How often should I bath my dog and what product should I use?

There are no fixed rules about how often a dog should be bathed. Some show dogs get washed every week without harmful effects, despite the old adage that you should only bath your dog every three months or so. If your dog has a good diet, constant washing will not remove all the oils out of its coat, but you do need to be careful about what product you use.

Basically, dogs should be bathed whenever they are dirty. Indoor pooches can be bathed weekly and if they still smell despite such frequent bathing, you need to consider either the environment the dog lives in, or the condition of the dog's skin. Check carefully to see if there is a problem in the coat or skin.

Skin inflammation caused by allergies will result in a malodorous skin due to the presence of bacteria. These dogs will require frequent bathing to remove the excess bacterial flora causing the smell. Bathing is also an adjunct to treatment for the allergy. Obviously the choice of product in these cases becomes even more critical as some shampoos will actively assist treatment while others exacerbate the problem.

Once you have decided your dog needs a wash, make sure it's a warm, sunny day then plan the task mid-morning to give the dog a good chance of drying. If you own a long-coated dog, drying with a hair dryer and brush will be essential for complete drying, while also ensuring you remove any mats in the coat. Since most dogs hate bathtime, don't call the dog over to a hose running with cold water — this will only make your dog disobedient. Place a soft collar around the neck, then walk your dog over to the bath site. Warm water is far more pleasant but dogs will tolerate cold water as long as it's a reasonable day without a chill in the air.

Dogs with normal skin — no excess dandruff or seborrhea — can be washed in most shampoos but be careful with harsher human products. Dogs' skin is covered with hair so it's far more sensitive than human skin, and some human anti-dandruff products, for example, will burn a dog's skin. There are many good, gentle shampoos with added natural products such as aloe vera, tea tree or even oatmeal. Some of these are sold with a conditioner, should you be worried that frequent bathing is drying out your dog's skin.

Dogs with dry, scaly skin or with excess dandruff can be bathed in the anti-seborrheic or anti-pruritic shampoos that are available for dogs or even some that are made for humans. Alpha Keri or Pinetarsol are commonly used to relieve itchiness in children (or adults), especially when they contract chicken pox, and the products are gentle and work well in some dogs. One of Australia's leading dermatologists always used sorbolene on his dog, which had a very shiny coat.

Dogs with moist eczema need regular washes in anti-bacterial shampoos to treat the skin while preventing excess bacterial build-up. Chlorhexidine, used by some surgeons to scrub clean before surgery, is common in many of these products. Also present in many of the canine shampoos are sulphur, salicylic acid and coal tar.

Anti-fungal agents that have recently been added to human shampoos are also present in dog washes. This has proved particularly successful in assisting dogs with chronic dermatitis. Chlorhexidine and miconazole have not only been an asset for people with dandruff, but in dogs it is marketed as a 'topical keratolytic, anti-bacterial, antifungal and anti-pruritic foam for dogs'. Basically it removes bugs and junk like scale and grease from your dog's skin while stopping the itching. In fact, so gentle is this preparation, the manufacture recommends that you can use it twice weekly.

Analyse this to work out how often to bath your dog:

1   Do you keep your dog outside because it smells?
2   Does your dog continually scratch?
3   As soon as you get out the shampoo, does your dog run away, hating the idea of being bathed because it's such an infrequent occurrence?
4   Is there dirt and loose hair on the dog's bedding?

Yes, to any of these questions means that you're not bathing the family pooch as frequently as needed.

52. What is the reddish-brown staining around the eyes, mouth and feet of my white dog?

Like so many other creatures, even humans, dogs have bacteria on their skin. These little critters are termed 'normal flora' and are bugs that normally live happily without doing any harm. If the conditions change, the number of these bacteria will alter, and leaving an area moist can proliferate bacteria. Add nutrients to the moisture, such as compounds found in many body fluids from the eyes, mouth or from sweat pores of a dog's feet, and the bacteria flourishes in a bloom that exudes other chemicals causing staining of white coat hair.

So how can the nasty staining caused by the over-growth of bacteria be controlled?

A good starting point is to wash the whole dog regularly. Consider a mild soap or shampoo with an antiseptic that can be utilised once or twice daily on the trouble spots. Bacteria usually do well in a more alkaline environment so it may help to decrease the pH of the secretions by giving daily doses of vitamin C (ascorbic acid). This can also be applied weekly to the stained areas, just before bathing, in the form of neat lemon juice. Let the lemon juice soak into the coat for a short time but be very careful around the eyes, making sure you don't splash any onto the eyeballs. It's best to use a cotton bud soaked in lemon juice to avoid damage to the eyes. Never leave the lemon juice in for longer than ten minutes as this can affect the skin.

Some people who show small white dogs such as Bichon Frise, Maltese or Shih tzu actually place their dogs on long-term low dosage antibiotics in an endeavour to minimise staining. This practice is outrageous and can only lead to the promotion of bacteria that are resistant to antibiotics. These antibiotic-resistant bugs are not only dangerous to the dogs but are a danger to all of us.

53. Should I have my dog's teeth cleaned? How often?

A dog should be taken to the vet to be anaesthetised and to have his teeth ultrasonically cleaned and scaled whenever there is an excessive build up of tartar or dental calculus on the teeth. This will cause offensive smelly breath and severe inflammation of the gums. The gum inflammation can be seen as a very red line at the junction of the gums and teeth. Left untreated, the gums retract from the teeth, ulcers form and the teeth loosen. Bacteria continue to build up in the mouth, until pus can be seen oozing from the gums whenever the area is pressed.

Individual dogs, however, will have different requirements for when they may require their teeth scaled by a vet. It all depends on breed, metabolism, the dog's diet and the degree of preventative care administered by owners.

Small breeds (toy dogs) usually require more dental care than larger breeds. Also the short-muzzled (brachycephalic) breeds require more dental care than dogs with longer muzzles. In both cases, dental crowding is one of the biggest issues affecting care of the dog's teeth. Owners need to pay particular attention in the first year of their dog's life that the milk teeth are all completely shed. If retained, these can lead to overcrowding, which causes food to be caught between the teeth, allowing a build-up of bacteria.

Metabolism plays a significant role because some animals of the same breed and on the same diet will vary in their need to have ultrasonic tooth scaling. Some dogs will produce more acidic saliva while others more alkaline saliva. There will also be a variation in the concentration of salts and calcium ions in the saliva itself. These ions are deposited on the teeth forming tartar, so varying concentrations will mean varying degree of build up of tartar.

Chewing bones a few times each week will greatly assist a dog's dental hygiene. Owners often make the mistake, especially with small breeds of dogs, of not offering bones when the animal is a young puppy. If puppies are not given the opportunity to chew bones from a very young age, as adults they will often ignore bones, waiting for their normal meal in preference to having to work their teeth. True, at a very young age the most a puppy will do to a bone is to give it a nasty suck – just remember that the puppy is learning a valuable lesson.

Never feed your dog chicken bones. Small dogs have been presented to veterinary clinics with pieces of chicken bone piercing through their intestinal tract and large dogs have been presented for swallowing whole chicken wings or chicken necks which cause blockage of the stomach outlet. By far the safest bones to use are raw mutton flaps or raw brisket bones. While bones should form part of the diet, a hard complete dry food, mixed with a little water but not soaked, should form the basis of the dog's daily ration.

If you do the basic things in looking after your dog's teeth, this can avoid the need to have the animal's teeth cleaned professionally. Some owners have taught their dogs to accept brushing of their teeth. As dogs tend to swallow the toothpaste, it is important that you buy special preparations through veterinary outlets. If your dog does not tolerate brushing of its teeth, then special dental gels can be placed in the mouth, which act by stimulating the correct pH and have a slight abrasive action on the teeth to remove plaque.

During your dog's annual visit for its yearly vaccinations, the vet should give it a full physical examination including the teeth. Plaque formation with subsequent tartar and gingivitis are very common and the yearly checkup is a good preventative measure. A severe infection of the roots and gums can result in the removal of all teeth. Allowing things to get this bad is nothing less than neglectful — with just a little care and scrutiny of the diet, the whole problem can be avoided.

54. Do my dog's ears need cleaning? How do I do it?

How often should you clean a dog's ears? Well, whenever they need cleaning. There's no set rule such as weekly or monthly because some dogs rarely need their ears cleaned while others require frequent cleaning. The signs that a dog needs its ears cleaned are smell from the ears, visible discharge (usually dark and oozy) and continual head shaking.

In most cases, cleaning ears can be performed successfully without a full anaesthetic, though some owners may require a tranquilliser! Titbits of food can be used as an incentive for your dog to cooperate, or to at least distract the animal from something it may perceive as unpleasant. Once dogs become accustomed to having their ears cleaned, they learn to accept this without undue protest.

Cleaning ears takes two people. One person needs to hold the head still, preventing the dog from shaking everything out just when it's doing the most good. Apart from a helper, you will also need a good quality ear cleaner and a roll of cotton wool. Cotton buds, q-tips, and swab sticks are all unnecessary and potentially harmful instruments with which to clean a pooch's ears.

Warm the ear cleaner slightly as there is nothing worse than cold fluid being introduced into the ear canal. To warm it, stand the container in hot water or give it a few seconds in the microwave, but make sure it isn't too hot. Flood the ear canal with the warmed cleaner, then gently massage. Do this for a few minutes until the wax and crud caught in the ear canal dislodges and rises to the top. Feed loose cotton wool into the canal then pull it out. The wax and grime will attach itself to the cotton fibres.

Do not turn the cotton wool around inside the ear canal in an endeavour to polish the canal clean. It's not silverware you're cleaning, and cotton wool inside an ear canal can be like sandpaper — so abrasive that it can do more harm than good. Repeat the process, again flooding the canal and feeding cotton wool down, then retrieving it until the cotton wool comes out clean.

If symptoms, especially head shaking, continue despite frequent cleaning then a trip to the vet is required. The dog may have bacterial, fungal or even parasitic infection in the ears.

If the ears become a chronic problem, it can be due to one of three causes. Infection deep in the membranes of the ears is not an uncommon occurrence but it can't be fixed by cleaning and the application of drops. Secondly, it may be that the dog that has small (stenotic) ear canals that do not allow good ventilation and so keep the area continually moist. Finally, it could reflect the fact that the dog has a chronic skin problem. Dogs with chronic dermatitis and who are fighting long-term allergy situations will often have associated ear infections. In these cases, the owner has to consider an ear re-section to give as much permanent relief as possible.

If ears need to be cleaned weekly then a clear diagnosis is required and your vet is the best person to do this. Ear mites, fungi, bacteria, even foreign bodies can all be the cause of a continually smelly, discharging ear canal. Treatment may involve ear drops but could also include oral antibiotics or perhaps an anaesthetic to remove a grass seed wedged in the ear drum or penetrating the side of the ear canal.

55. Should I cut my dog's nails, and if so, how?

Some dogs, especially if they have the correct foot shape and get exercise on a rough surface such as gravel or even concrete, wear their own nails down to the level at which they should be maintained. Nail cutting is required when a dog makes a click, click sound when walking on hard smooth surfaces — a dog should walk on its pads not its nails.

You need good quality nail clippers, cotton wool, cotton buds and a blood-clotting powder or stick, similar to the type used to stop bleeding from a shaving wound. Make sure you have the right equipment: garden secateurs or shears and other such implements will crush the nail causing pain rather than giving a clean cut.

Dogs have a nerve and a blood vessel inside each of their nails and if these are severed the dog will bleed and experience pain. Dogs with black nails are at more risk of being hurt during a nail trimming because the blood vessel cannot be seen through the nail. Clear nails can even have a torch light shone through them to establish the exact position of the blood vessel. Trim well in front of this to ensure you also avoid cutting through the nerve. If you are uncertain, walk on the side of caution and just take the tips off the nails. You can always come back and do the same in a week or so. With dogs that have long nails, regular trimming pushes the blood vessel and nerve back so the nails can be kept respectably short.

If you do cut a blood vessel, don't panic — it's not the end of the world. The blood vessel will pump blood out making a mess that looks worse than it really is. Hold some cotton wool on the nail so that the blood can clot. Better still, place a wet cotton bud into the blood-clotting powder then hold this on the bleeding nail surface and the bleeding will stop within seconds.

56. Is it okay to clip my long-coated dog myself, and if so, how?

Have a good look at and feel of your dog. If you can feel large lumps of matted hair or you can see debris and knots through the coat, it may pay to have one last professional clip and groom before you take on this responsibility. Set aside one whole day for your first attempt at sprucing up your dog. It may not take quite this long but rushing might result in an expensive trip to the vet to patch your poor dog's skin. It may also help to have an assistant for physical (and emotional) support.

Electric clippers will be the most expensive capital outlay. Don't skimp: cheap clippers will quickly break down. Spend extra to buy a decent set of clippers and purchase an extra blade. The size of blade required is around a ten or twenty, but size may vary with brand so check with the sales person.

You need a table or workbench with a non-slip surface. You might want to purchase a rubber mat for this purpose or use some old towels. If your dog has been to the groomers before, it will be used to being on a table. Little titbits fed to the dog while it's on the table will make it a better experience. Having it at waist height will save your back.

If your dog is not used to clippers, turn them on while feeding the dog a tasty morsel of food on the table. This will allow the dog time to adjust to the noise. Next, while still feeding, start clipping the hair from the least matted area. The sides, along the back and even the tummy are relatively easy. The head region, especially around the eyes and over the ears is more difficult and care is needed not to hurt the dog or damage the skin as you clip the hair away. Finally, the feet present a challenge because the majority of dogs are ticklish around their feet. You must remove the matted hair between the toes.

Take it slowly when you clip, doing small strokes to avoid clogging the blade. Two tips for making your clippers easier to use:

- Old toothbrushes are excellent to keep the blades clean.
- Spray blades with a lubricant (either special blade oil or even a short burst with WD40).
- Once the dog's hair is removed check the ears to see if they need cleaning and look at the nails in case they need a trim. At this point, a professional grooming salon might well check the anal glands! Not a pleasant experience for you or the dog, but if you are up to it, see pages 118–119.

At last, it's bath time. Use a good quality dog shampoo that suits your dog's skin. Remember, your dog is now separated from its insulation coat, leaving it more exposed to temperatures and sunburn. Shade, sunblock, a coat and possibly lots more time indoors may be required to avoid stress to your friend.

57. Is insurance essential for my dog?

Pet health insurance may not be essential for your dog but it's feasible that your pet's life could swing in the balance without it some day. Many an owner has been forced to make the decision to euthanise the family dog because they don't have the funds to cover an expensive life-saving procedure. A dog hit by a car might need emergency therapy that could easily amount to several thousand dollars. Treatment to save a dog bitten by a snake will easily cost over a thousand dollars. Pet health insurance can prove more than a little handy especially in unexpected circumstances.

If you do decide to purchase pet health insurance, you have to do your homework. Check out what each policy covers for what cost, but also see how long they have been in the market — many insurance companies have entered the area of pet insurance but few have stayed.

The other type of insurance is a public risk policy and you should seriously consider this. Far too many people have literally lost their homes to pay costs when their dog has caused human suffering.

It's easy to imagine the loss and injury suffered by someone if they are severely attacked by a dog. Apart from hospital expenses, the person may not be able to work for some time as a result of the attack. Psychological suffering could see the person housebound for months or even years.

But, you say, your dog would never bite anyone! A meek, mild-mannered animal may not bite but it could easily wrap a lead around a stranger's legs causing a nasty fall. Check with your insurance broker or company about cover for your dog biting someone, both on or off your property, or causing an accident. The cover needed should involve lots of zeros before the decimal point — it's not just peoples' lives we're talking about, lawyers will also have to be paid!

58. What should I keep in the medicine cupboard for my dog?

The first thing to have in an emergency kit for your dog is a large dose of calmness — this will avert panic if anything terrible happens.

Many types of bandages are available on pharmacy shelves, but all you need is a crepe bandage and a roll of cotton wool and conforming gauze. The best type of crepe is the self-adhesive variety (it clings to itself) which can be purchased from vets and pet shops as 'vet wrap'. The main uses of bandages in a dog first aid kit will be to wrap an area that is bleeding excessively, to keep an open wound clean or to support a broken limb. In all instances, veterinary assistance must be sought immediately but good first aid could save your dog's life.

Wounds can be cleaned with a mixture of water or saline combined with equal parts with hydrogen peroxide. Therefore, sterile saline and 3% hydrogen peroxide should be in your kit. Saline can also be used to flush eyes if ever they're inflamed or have any toxin splashed in them. Betadine should also be in the emergency cupboard as this can be used to kill bugs that might otherwise infect a wound. Simply douse the Betadine into the wound before covering the area.

A common problem in dogs is a swollen face resulting from a bee sting. This is often seen in spring and summer when more bees are out doing their work — some dogs have a habit of chasing bees around the garden. Antihistamines are very useful to treat this condition if it is caught early. However, if the face is severely swollen, breathing may become compromised so that the animal needs cortisone injections administered by a vet to get the condition under control quickly.

Aspirin can be helpful if a soft tissue injury is sustained by a dog, resulting in lameness and pain. A dose of 10 to 20 mg per kilogram can help with musculoskeletal pain (arthritis) or even acute lameness. Never, under any circumstances, use paracetamol on dogs as this can permanently destroy their liver.

One of the most common complaints seen by vets in dogs is diarrhoea. This usually reflects the fact that dogs tend to scavenge, thereby eating things that are less than wholesome. But it may also reflect the fact that we feed our dogs incorrectly — too much food, too often. Regardless of the cause, a good gastrointestinal compound such as 'Kaomagma' can be very useful. It acts to absorb bacterial toxins from the gut while increasing the bulk of the droppings. Basically, it is good symptomatic relief of non-specific diarrhoea, while appropriate rehydration therapy can be given concurrently.

Skin irritations are also a common occurrence, especially in hot climates with lots of vegetation and insects. Dermatitis is often noticed by owners because the dogs continually scratch, never getting much relief. Usually such cases are best treated by your local vet who is taught to assess the cause of the allergy. However, there are some basic things you can try at home to relieve itching, at least in the short term. Simple, old-fashioned compounds are often useful to give some relief. Pinetarsol or Alpha Keri washes, which are used to relieve such problems as chicken pox, can often help dogs' skin. Sprays that are cooling, such as those containing witch hazel, will often give quick alleviation of symptoms, and antihistamines may help until you can consult your vet.

Ear cleaners and ear drops recommended by your vet are often a useful addition to your dog's medicine chest. It might stop a dog shaking and scratching his head if an acute earache occurs.

A thermometer is possibly another item you should include in your dog's medicine cupboard but remember to use it just for your dog. Taking a pup's temperature involves holding the animal still for a few minutes while the thermometer is gently inserted into its rectum for one minute. A dog's normal rectal temperature is between 37.5°C and 39°C.

Electrolyte supplements are also handy in a first aid kit as these can be used routinely on hot days. A cool drink with electrolytes can go a long way towards making them more comfortable. These can be purchased through any veterinary outlet but if none are available, don't forget the basic supplements available in supermarkets for human use — they can be equally effective on your dog.

Ipecac is a mixture which makes dogs (and people) vomit. As dogs are the most likely animal to ingest poisons, such a mixture can be valuable. If you see your dog ingest snail bait or rat poison, immediate action with Ipecac could save your pet's life.

A 24-hour number for a veterinary service is essential because there are many emergencies that require prompt veterinary action. If you are ever in doubt about your dog's health, contact your vet immediately.

59. How do I give my dog a tablet?

I once made a house call to an elderly gentleman whose dog had diarrhoea. It seemed a simple case so I prescribed the appropriate tablets, confident that the problem would quickly subside. A couple of days later he telephoned to say the tablets weren't working. Asked if the dog was taking the tablets all right, the old man replied, 'I put them in but he immediately poos them out.'

So, the first thing to note about medication is that you must read the instructions carefully. If you don't understand the instructions, ask the vet or the veterinary nurse.

Administering medication to a dog isn't always simple. Puppies will struggle, often leading to bad habits with the dog clamping up, ready for a fight rather than taking tablets. Disguising tablets is the best option. A covering with butter, or better still, liverwurst, pate or cheese, will go a long way to teaching your dog that taking medication can be enjoyable. Most dogs will swallow tablets whole when they are disguised in something they like.

Dogs that protest regardless of the presentation of their medication have to be handled firmly. It's yet another case of controlling the head so you control the beast, as the old saying says. Sit the dog in a corner, lift its head towards the ceiling, and then place your thumb and middle finger of the hand holding the head, at the end of the lower jaw. Push the lower jaw down, then place your hand with the tablet inside the open mouth. You must get the tablet as far back as possible. Take your hand out, close the jaw but always ensure the dog's nose is facing upwards. Rub the neck where it reaches the lower jaw. You can feel the enlargement of the voice box or Adam's apple (called the larynx) in this region. Once you see or feel the dog swallow, let the head relax and see if your dog manages to spit the tablet back out!

If all this fails after repeated attempts, a fluid form of the same medication may be required. Like administering tablets, the head still needs to be controlled but the mouth doesn't have to be forced open. The liquid can be slowly and carefully syringed into the mouth in a gap between the teeth. Once the fluid has been administered, hold the head up for several seconds so that gravity will take it to the back of the throat. The dog will then be forced to swallow it.

60. Do natural remedies work?

Herbal medicines have been around for centuries, and really are where modern medicine started. Even today, many new medicines are derived from herbal compounds. Recently, scientists isolated a chemical compound inside New Zealand green-lipped mussels that assists in treating inflamed joints. Herbalists had been using the same extract for decades.

A prime example of the possible benefits of herbal medicines for dogs is shown in a study in Australia of Bedlington terriers. An entire population of these dogs were found to be affected by a condition called 'copper toxicosis'. This is when the shut-off mechanism for adequate copper storage in the liver fails. The liver continues storing higher and higher levels of copper, causing heavy metal poisoning of the liver, resulting in severe debilitating symptoms. The recognised treatment for humans with this condition was found to have a negative effect on dogs. A treatment group of the terriers was placed onto St Mary's thistle (or milk thistle) extract. After one month of therapy, the liver enzymes of this group were nearly back to normal and all animals were clinically healthy. In this trial a herbal remedy, St Mary's thistle, had definite benefits in improving liver function.

As in so many debates, the truth as to whether herbal medicines are useful or not falls somewhere in the middle. Utilising them exclusively and attempting such things as 'herbal vaccinations' can ultimately result in the death of some animals. Ignoring them totally and relying exclusively on western medicine will mean your dog is missing out on some potential benefits, while possibly developing undesirable side effects from potent drugs.

Used in moderation, in conjunction with expert help, herbal medicines can improve the quality of life for your dog.

61. Does acupuncture work?

For many years, the very positive effects of acupuncture have baffled western scientists. Yet the evidence was clear when certain chronically painful spinal or joint conditions displayed a positive response after acupuncture therapy.

In humans, there is an actual notion of 'chi', a warm, numb or even uncomfortable feeling at the acupuncture site when stimulated by whatever means, be it needle, heat, vacuum, electrical stimulus, laser or other means. Since the discovery of beta-endorphins, hormones released by the body when the acupuncture site is stimulated, scientists appear more accepting of this ancient method of therapy.

As there are over three hundred acupuncture points, it is imperative that you seek an operator with some legitimate training in this field. The points do have an area of low electrical resistance which can be verified with a galvanometer or 'acupoint finder'.

However, it's not just a matter of finding the acupuncture point: you need to know exactly what area of the body is affected when this point is stimulated. For example, a point called 'Tsu San Li' which is found below the knee, can have a direct effect on heart and even gastrointestinal motility when stimulated.

Acupuncture has not only been used for treatment of chronic joint pain but has even assisted in ameliorating or even curing dysfunction of several organic systems. It has been used in cases of infertility, idiopathic vomiting and even eczema. Not all cases respond, but that is also true of western medicine.

62. How can I cure my dog of ringworm?

This fungal skin infection has been given the misleading name of 'ringworm' and people commonly make the error of thinking this condition is some kind of parasite like roundworm or threadworm. The circular skin legions caused by this fungus were thought to occur because of a worm actually curling up in the tissues. Some worms can infect skin, but the cause of ringworm is one of four fungi that can affect dogs. Once a dog becomes infected, spores from the fungus spread over the dog's body and all through the environment where it can infect humans and other animals. Adult humans are more resistant to infection, but children, whose immune system is yet to develop, are commonly affected by this fungal skin problem.

The spores can live in the environment for several months and when conditions are right, hot and moist, the spores hatch, infecting the skin of any susceptible animal that they come into contact with. Despite aggressive treatment, pets can remain contagious for about three weeks. If treatment is neither swift nor intensive, your pet could remain contagious for an even longer period. Treatments must have four components.

Firstly, your vet will most likely prescribe a long course of oral anti-fungal drugs. The most commonly utilised drug is griseofulvin and this is given for a minimum of 30 days, but no matter what drug is prescribed, it is imperative that you follow directions and you administer the complete course.

Secondly, some form of topical anti-fungal drug should be directly applied to each lesion, old or new. This can be as simple as iodine, which is a good anti-fungal compound. Or it may be a more complex cream, lotion or spray prescribed by your vet.

Thirdly, frequent bathing with an anti-fungal shampoo can greatly assist in decreasing the spread of ringworm. There are many shampoos in this category, everything from chlorhexidine-based through to iodine-based washes, which are all very effective as they assist in the arrest of new, small lesions that have yet to lose hair. In the first week of treatment, bath every alternate day, then twice weekly for a fortnight and finally weekly for the next month.

The fourth problem that needs to be aggressively addressed is the dog's immediate environment. Blankets and bedding need to be soaked and washed in an anti-fungal disinfectant. This should occur weekly until the outbreak of the fungus appears contained. Diluted bleach is very effective and this can be sprayed in a kennel area or mopped over the floor and furniture being careful to avoid carpet and fabric. If the dog lies on carpet, then a fabric disinfectant that is fungicidal needs to be used weekly. Spores from ringworm are hardy and able to live in the environment for many months.

Recently, two vets working in Israel, evaluated a new drug, lufenuron, as an anti-fungal agent. They found that a single dose of this drug effected resolution of gross lesions within two to three weeks in dogs and even less time in cats. Considering the complexity of aggressive treatment against ringworm to date, lufenuron is bound to be a big boost in curing this hideous disease in the future.

63. My dog keeps coughing. What can I do?

This question is a common one for vets all over the world. It can sound as if an a foreign body is stuck in the dog's throat, but this very rarely is the cause of a cough. By far the most likely cause of a dog coughing is a highly infectious, upper respiratory disease, commonly known as kennel cough. It also sounds like whooping cough in children and in fact, one of the organisms causing this syndrome is related to the pertussis bug (whooping cough organism) that can affect kids. The disease causes severe inflammation of the upper airways, especially the windpipe or trachea. So painful is the dog's throat that every time cold air hits this region, the dog will react to the irritation by coughing and sometimes bringing up white phlegm. People notice the dog coughing during the cold nights or first thing in the morning.

Two organisms are involved in causing kennel cough. The first bug is a virus called parainfluenza. The second nasty is a bacteria-like organism called *Bordetella bronchisepta*. They can either act individually to bring about the symptoms, or in worse cases they attack the cells of the upper airways together.

Without treatment, the disease can last much longer and result in permanent damage to the trachea, leaving such bad scar tissue that the dog is continually short of breath and unable to run long distances. It is therefore wise to instigate treatment at the commencement of symptoms rather than waiting.

Your vet will make a diagnosis of kennel cough or viral tracheal bronchitis based on the history and clinical signs. There is no specific symptom that allows a definite diagnosis, but because of the very inflamed upper respiratory tract, a cough can be elicited by palpation of the wind pipe.

Treatment in the initial stages involves keeping the animal warm especially during the evening and early morning. Broad spectrum antibiotics are prescribed and a good cough syrup eases inflammation of the throat. In severe cases, steam therapy is used to break up mucus.

Vaccines are available for both the viral cause and the bordetella organism. Vaccination for this complex disease is compulsory for animals going into kennels and recommended for all dogs. Just like human flu viruses, different types occur, so even vaccinated dogs can develop symptoms of kennel cough. Generally dogs that have been vaccinated and still manage to contract kennel cough recover quickly, and very rarely become severe cases resulting in pneumonia.

In a household where a dog develops the symptoms of kennel cough, it is imperative that children, especially those under five, are separated from the dog. During the early stages of the disease the dog will shed many virus particles which will become airborne. They can easily affect a child with a developing immune system.

64. Can dogs be epileptics?

A seizure, or fit, refers to involuntary, uncontrollable muscular activity and occurs because of some disturbance of the brain sending uncoordinated messages to the muscles to contract. A dog undergoing a seizure usually cannot stand up, moves all its legs as if trying to run, may bark or cry out and will often urinate or defecate. Epilepsy refers to the recurrence of seizures. The dog will usually function normally between seizures, however, if they are continuous, the condition is then called 'status epilepticus'. In dogs, the most common seizure is the grand mal seizure where all the muscles are affected. Petit mal seizures occur when there is some loss of consciousness and small muscle tremors but these are relatively rare in dogs.

Epilepsy is not easy to diagnose in dogs because diagnostic aids commonly used in humans are both expensive and difficult to access in the veterinary field. The diagnosis is made on the owner's history of the dog and a thorough physical examination that rules out any diseases that may adversely affect the brain. The vet must eliminate the possibility of other causes of seizures before a final diagnosis of epilepsy can be made.

A dog with poor heart function could develop seizures when blood pressure to the brain is compromised. Diabetes can often result in seizures, as can an infection to the brain or its surrounding tissues (encephalitis or meningitis). These, and other causes such as poor liver function or toxins (for example, lead poisoning), must all be excluded as possible reasons for the seizures. A variety of tests are available but the cost of these can be expensive, so providing a thorough history may assist in decreasing the need to explore every test.

The vet may make a tentative diagnosis of epilepsy in a dog that has had more than one seizure, but otherwise appears perfectly healthy. In doing so, the dog may enter a therapy trial. If the dog shows a good response to an anti-epileptic drug regime then it is reasonable to presume that the seizure may have arisen from an unknown cause.

The cause of epilepsy is not totally clear. While there is obviously a possibility of genetic epilepsy occurring, such things as lack of oxygen to the brain during birth, trauma to the brain by a blow or accident or even a transient toxicity to any region of the brain could all result in a pattern of intermittent seizures. Even an extremely small, benign tumour or small blood clot (brain infarction) could cause seizure activity in the brain.

The treatment is the same in all cases. Therapy endeavours to remove the seizures without affecting the animal's level of consciousness. There is a vast range of anti-epilepsy drugs, all of which will have some degree of side effects on your dog.

Drug therapy cannot cure your dog and most will still have some seizures. The therapy can decrease the number of fits a patient must endure as well as decreasing the severity of each seizure. Prior to a seizure, many dogs change behaviour drastically, often clinging to owners or anyone who is around. Alternatively, they can become uncharacteristically aggressive. These changes are also noted in human epileptics and the phase is called the 'aura' — somehow the epileptic knows a seizure is coming. Owners should become aware of these changes in behaviour and act immediately by giving the dog a large dose of anti-convulsive drug, thereby avoiding a seizure.

It's a big commitment owning an epileptic animal. You need to either be there or, for those times when you can't be at home, arrange for someone to administer medication so that regular dosing can be fulfilled. The balance you are trying to achieve for your dog is minimal seizures while maintaining a normal lifestyle.

65. Can dogs have a kidney transplant?

There are several reasons why, although medically possible, organ transplantation in dogs rarely occurs outside research facilities.

- Monetary considerations. Expenses for patient monitoring, medication (immunosuppressive therapy), along with the cost of accessing donors would be high let alone the direct cost of transplantation.
- Cost of veterinary hospitals acquiring and maintaining the specialised equipment required.
- Possibility of failure.
- Limited facilities for donor/recipient matching.

But of all these considerations perhaps the ethical reason is the single, strongest limiting factor. Should a healthy donor be placed through major surgery? If the donor dog is unknown to the recipient animal, would the donor dog willingly submit to the surgery if it had a free choice?

No doubt there are cases where dogs, brought up together, fret to the point of their own demise of the death of a partner. One amazing case was reported when a horse died and its mate refused to eat for several days then laid in a dam to drown. Despite desperate attempts by the owner to pull the animal out, it refused to be saved, committing suicide rather than living without its lifelong friend. Such instances have also been seen in other species of animals including the dog. But most dogs do not have a life partner and even if they did, it would be rare for it to be an ideal donor.

So where do we access a donor for an ailing pet? One consideration might be a pound but the donor would need to be anaesthetised, the organ removed, and then the animal would be euthanised. One may argue that this dog was to be killed anyway and that its life was at least used to save another. But did the donor suffer in the process? Was it scared, taken from a pound to a hospital where the anaesthetic was eventually delivered? Did the animal have to die at all?

Despite all these ethical questions and more, there is anticipation that kidney transplantation will become more available in the next decade.

66. Can a dog be diabetic?

Absolutely. 'Sugar' diabetes (diabetes mellitus) occurs reasonably often in dogs over six years of age.

Just like humans with the disease, these dogs have low insulin levels. Insulin opens the gates into cells which allows sugar (glucose) to enter the cells. When insulin is low, sugar cannot enter the cell and so the cell becomes starved of its energy source. To overcome this effect, the body begins to break down stores of fat and protein and so the dog loses weight and has a ravenous appetite. In the meantime, the glucose that has not been able to get into the cells builds up in the bloodstream. The glucose attracts water, so large quantities of fluid are removed from the body, which results in copious urine production. To avoid dehydration the dog drinks excessively.

The four classic signs of diabetes begin to occur with increasing intensity:
- weight loss
- ravenous appetite
- increased urine production
- large water intake

A vet is required to make the definitive diagnosis by measuring the glucose in the urine and in the blood. If it is high, then the only form of treatment is daily insulin injections. To prevent a diabetic crisis, insulin injections and a feeding regime must be scheduled within strict daily time limits.

If you find that you become the owner of a diabetic dog, you need to consider all options. You can be taught to give injections, you can be given instructions on a feeding routine, you can even be taught how to monitor your dog; but you need to ask yourself, are you prepared to put in the effort, time and money to keep your dog alive?

67. Can dogs get cancer?

Cancer cells are broadly divided into either benign or malignant. Benign cells grow slowly and cause small lumps that can be found anywhere and are not uncommon under or even on the skin itself. Generally tumours that arise from benign cancer cells do little harm unless they happen to grow in an extremely sensitive and important region such as the brain. As dogs become older, over eight years of age, benign tumours are more common. Often determined by the shape, location and rate of growth, benign tumours are usually left alone and not removed from the body as the risks involved in a general anaesthetic are greater than the risk from a benign tumour itself.

Tumours arising from malignant cells present an entirely different scenario. These tumours grow rapidly in size. They damage the organs they infiltrate and have the capability of a few cells breaking off from the original tumour mass then travelling through the body to find other locations in which to grow and ultimately damage. Either because of the destruction of a vital organ or the multiple areas of damage caused by malignant tumours, an affected animal will eventually die if treatment is not effective. Treatment can be painful and expensive. Your vet will help you to decide whether the treatment is practical and affordable in your pet's specific situation.

Some malignant cancers, such as those stemming from thyroid cells, are very successfully treated by administering radioactive iodine to the patient. Malignant thyroid cells have a greedy need for iodine and suck up any radioactive iodine that may be in the body. The radioactivity in the iodine destroys the cell, ultimately killing off all the cancer. However, a malignant bone tumour with multiple secondary growths throughout the body, especially in the lungs, would be deemed untreatable by your vet. All that could be offered is palliative care in an attempt to keep your dog pain-free and as happy for as long as possible.

The decision on whether a malignant tumour or cancer is considered treatable will depend upon many medical considerations: the type of cancer cell, the current state of the dog's health, the availability of professional help and access to the correct drugs or other therapeutic requirements. Very often therapy may not lead to total cure of animals with cancer. However, it is possible that many cases can be placed into remission for at least a couple of years.

Cancer therapy is aimed at killing off malignant cancer cells, but healthy cells are inadvertently destroyed in the process. This is why undesirable side effects occur during cancer therapy. A specialist or at least someone experienced with the various processes involved in killing off cancer cells can tell you what to expect by way of side effects for your dog.

Early detection gives your dog the best chance to recover from a malignant cancer. Any lump or bump, unusual lethargy, sudden weight loss or even unusual behaviour may all be attributable to cancer. Learn what is normal, be observant of any abnormalities and give your dog the best opportunity for a quick recovery.

68. What is pancreatitis?

Pancreatitis is an extremely serious disease. It is the inflammation of the pancreas. This small but very vital organ is found just beneath the stomach at the beginning of the intestinal tract. The pancreas has two functions. Its best known task is to release insulin inside the bloodstream to control the body's blood sugar level. The second function is to release enzymes into the intestinal tract for the digestion of particular ingredients in food, especially the proteins.

Pancreatitis results in severe abdominal pain causing the animal to walk with a hunched back and experience sudden bouts of vomiting and severe diarrhoea. Because of the relationship of the pancreas to the intestinal tract, inflammation in this area can result in bacteria and toxins entering the bloodstream. This can result in endotoxic shock that kills the dog in a very short period of time. If pancreatitis is suspected, immediate veterinary attention must be sought.

Your vet will admit an animal suspected of pancreatitis to hospital so that proper therapy can take place. Intravenous fluids are essential in flushing the system of toxins and other supportive drugs such as anti-inflammatories and antibiotics will be administered. A blood test will also be performed to determine if your dog is suffering from this condition but your vet will not wait for the result to instigate therapy for this condition — after all, your dog's life hangs in the balance. Food and water are withdrawn, possibly for a period of three to five days, making the intravenous fluids an essential part of treatment. Hospitalisation is unavoidable.

It is uncertain what precipitates a bout of pancreatitis, but most certainly very rich food or foods that are extremely high in fats can lead to the condition. Bones that have a great deal of fat on them can lead to pancreatitis. Most certainly dogs that have suffered the condition must remain on a lean diet for the rest of their lives. Obesity is another common factor found in dogs suffering from pancreatitis.

Other causes relate to such things as bacterial or viral infections, especially in dogs that are prone to eating foodstuff with high levels of bacteria.

The pain from a bout of acute pancreatitis can cause a dog to lose consciousness and collapse. It cannot be over stressed that dogs that have the signs of pancreatitis, that is vomiting, diarrhoea, severe gut pain and possibly a fever, must be presented to a vet as quickly as possible as their lives are in danger.

69. Can dogs get cataracts?

An old dog's eyes can become a bit blue or cloudy but this is not likely to be cataracts. It is called nuclear sclerosis, which is a hardening of the lens that occurs with age. This affliction does cause some change in the way light is refracted through the eye, but in the majority of cases it does not lead to blindness. Humans have the same changes as they get older — the lens becomes harder, making focusing at shorter distance more difficult, which is why we may need to wear reading glasses as we age. As dogs do little reading, very often the bluey lenses are of little consequence to the dog's sight or health. Most dogs manage quite well until they die from old age.

That is not to say that dogs can't get cataracts. Cataracts are clouding of the lenses with the pupils initially becoming milky and then turning white. Light cannot get through, rendering the animal totally blind once the cataract has fully formed.

Cataracts can develop because of pathology or disease to the eye, or can be inherited. Metabolic diseases, such as sugar diabetes, are well know for producing cataracts but anything that can cause severe inflammation of the eye can cause cataracts.

Cataracts in dogs can be removed, however, it is pointless performing surgical removal of cataracts if other areas of the eye are not sound and healthy. A specialist ophthalmologist would therefore need to check the eyes and the dog's overall health would be examined. Cataract surgery requires extremely specialised equipment and a highly trained medical team. Consequently, such surgery comes at a price so you need to make sure that you understand what is involved before you elect to embark on surgical correction of cataracts.

If inherited cataracts, or indeed any other inherited eye diseases, are common in the breed you have chosen, then do not purchase a puppy without sighting certificates from a specialised ophthalmologist clearing both parents for the disease. Better still, if a DNA test is available you should sight not only the DNA tests for the parents but most importantly a DNA test for the puppy you are about to purchase. The test certificate should be matched with positive identification such as a tattoo or microchip number. If DNA analysis is available, then this can give you absolute assurance as to whether your pup could develop inherited cataracts. It does not of course mean that your dog could not develop acquired cataracts, but such an issue simply cannot be avoided. It is simply a sad possibility of life.

Not all dogs with cataracts need necessarily undergo surgery. Dogs, especially those living inside under close human supervision, are amenable to living their life with fully mature cataracts, unable to see but relying on other senses. If you elect to live with a blind dog, then it's a good idea to not rearrange the furniture too often. Dogs soon learn where obstacles are to be found and can avoid them without undue trauma. They also learn where stairs are and can negotiate these without any problems, relying on their sense of smell, hearing and touch to direct them through a safe, confined yard.

70. Do dogs get headaches? Can they have paracetamol?

I have never been able to find anyone that can answer the question about headaches in dogs or other domestic animals for that matter. Many of the known causes of headaches for humans are most certainly possibilities for dogs. Yet the perplexing questions remain: do dogs suffer headaches and, if so, how do we know when they have one?

If you live in a close relationship with your dog or if you work with dogs on a regular basis, you must undoubtedly observe that from time to time your dog may have an inexplicably bad day — a day when they are just out of sorts. A day when you begin to question your dog's intelligence or your training methods.

We come to expect particular habits and behaviour patterns from our dogs so that when they don't occur we simply believe the dog is being bad or testing the limits of training and relationship. The dog will go for a walk with you, even chase a ball, canter around the park if that's what you want to do, or involve itself in any of the daily rituals that you normally expect it to perform. Its usual enthusiasm for these however, to the observant owner, might not be up to the average daily standard. On these days the dog may not want to eat, will sleep more often, seek quieter sheltered corners and even be seen to squint somewhat in bright light. The next day the dog snaps out of it. But what has passed through it? Virus? Bacteria? Some form of infection or metabolic disease? Or did the dog simply have a headache?

When we begin to feel out of sorts we often reach for a bottle of paracetamol — it can help bring down a fever, relieve pain and can certainly assist with headaches, so why not give some to the dog? Stop right there. In dogs, paracetamol can lead to severe injury in the liver. Continuous use of paracetamol or one large dose given to your dog can cause it to continually vomit, develop diarrhoea, become jaundiced (yellowing of all the membranes, particularly noticeable in the whites of the eye) and even lead to seizures and eventually death of the animal. This does not mean that the drug is unsafe for humans. It simply reflects the inability of the canine species to metabolise it.

If your dog seems to have some non-specific pain, and you elect to try some home remedies before attending a veterinary hospital, then aspirin can be useful. Non-specific pain might include headache, or some joint soreness, or the dog might have a fever because of a mild virus. The dose rate for aspirin is 10 mg per kilogram of body weight, which means that the average 300 mg tablet does a 30 kg dog. If necessary the dose can be repeated every 12 hours, but you do need to seek veterinary advice if the therapy needs to be continued for any length of time. Be aware that too much aspirin can cause small ulcerations in the intestines, which lead to dark, loose bowel movements or vomiting — if these symptoms are seen then you definitely need to get your dog to a vet.

71. What is Cushing's syndrome?

Cushing's syndrome, or hyperadrenocorticism, is a condition in which there is too much cortisone in the bloodstream. The clinical signs include a bloated abdomen, excess drinking, continuous appetite and, as the disease progresses, hair loss, thinning of the skin and weakening of muscles and ligaments. In many circumstances, owners fail to realise there is any problem because the disease progresses slowly. This insidious nature of the disease, combined with the fact that it occurs in old animals, fools owners into thinking that the symptoms are that of old age rather than the chronic elevation of blood cortisol.

There are three main reasons for increased cortisone in the blood. The most common reason for chronically high blood cortisone is a functional tumor located in the pituitary gland. This gland is the control centre of all hormones in the body. The functional tumour produces a hormone that stimulates the adrenal glands located near the kidneys to produce continuous high levels of cortisone.

A second reason for Cushing's syndrome is an increase in the size of the adrenal glands. This form of hyperadrenocorticism is far less common, accounting for only ten per cent of Cushing's cases. It is seen more frequently in poodles than in other breeds.

Finally, the disease can be induced by the long-term, daily administration of large doses of cortisone for the treatment of other diseases such as allergic skin problems or osteoarthritis.

A conclusive diagnosis of Cushing's syndrome can be difficult. Your vet cannot rely on clinical signs alone and a blood screen will assist in pointing towards an eventual diagnosis. Your vet will interpret the blood test, examining the amount and type of white cells in the blood as well as looking for changes in blood glucose levels and an increase in liver enzymes. A more definitive test is called a dexamethasone suppression test, where the dog's blood cortisol level is measured, then an injection of dexamethasone is given and the blood cortisol remeasured eight hours later. In normal dogs this drug, dexamethasone, will greatly reduce the blood cortisol level.

Treatment for Cushing's syndrome can be difficult as there are considerable differences in individual dogs' sensitivity to the drug utilised to treat this condition. The drug is given daily for five to ten days, while monitoring the dog closely for improvement of such symptoms as excess water intake. Once the water intake decreases markedly the daily administration ceases and a maintenance dose of the drug is given weekly in an attempt to prevent recurrence. These weekly doses must continue for the life of the animal, otherwise the problem will commence again.

In very old dogs with Cushing's syndrome, owners need to decide whether to undertake therapy. The drug used to treat the condition has its own set of side effects, including gastrointestinal irritation leading to vomiting and anorexia, and even some disturbances of the nervous system so that the dog cannot walk properly and fails to coordinate all its legs correctly.

If Cushing's syndrome has been induced by the rarer cause, a functional adrenal tumour, surgery may be undertaken to remove this problem and to try to stop the spread of cancerous cells.

72. What is Addison's disease?

Seen more commonly in young to middle-aged dogs, Addison's disease, or hypoadrenocorticism, is the lack of cortisone in the bloodstream. Cortisone is manufactured in the body by the two glands near the kidneys known as adrenal glands. These glands can shut down the manufacture of cortisone for the body for many reasons although the exact cause of primary adrenal gland failure is often not known. Auto-immune disease, where the body attacks its own cell structure (in this case the adrenal gland) has been implicated. Other causes such as interruption of the blood supply by a blood clot, tumours or haemorrhage have also been seen as possible reasons for adrenal gland shutdown.

Another cause of adrenal gland shutdown is long-term, high doses of cortisone in tablet or injectable form. When the body receives continuous doses of cortisone from the outside, the need for the adrenal gland to produce cortisone decreases. Given enough cortisone from the outside, the adrenal glands stop production. Then, when this outside cortisone is suddenly withdrawn, an Addisonian crisis results.

The symptoms of chronic adrenal insufficiency are not always specific but include recurrent episodes of gastroenteritis, loss of body condition, often a very slow heart rate, kidney failure and sometimes even cardiovascular collapse. With an acute crisis, that is an extremely sudden decline in blood cortisone levels, a medical emergency arises with the animal often vomiting and passing vast amounts of blood. Such cases need immediate veterinary attention.

Once the crisis period has passed, oral therapy can be utilised to maintain Addisonian cases. Depending upon the cause of the disease, some dogs do appear to restart their adrenal function so that they can maintain reasonably normal levels of blood cortisol themselves. However, the oral medication must be removed in a very slow fashion, weaning the dog off the tablets over a period of time.

Careful monitoring is obviously needed to avoid a crisis situation.

Dogs with this condition cannot cope with stress so care must be taken to avoid stressful situations. Dogs with Addison's disease should not be bred from as this can place the bitch at risk and puppies would be genetically predisposed to developing the condition.

73. Can dogs have thyroid problems?

Hypothyroidism is when the thyroid gland does not produce enough of a hormone called thyroxin, the active form of which is referred to as T4 in most mammals. This slows down a dog's metabolism and causes weight gain, a decrease in exercise tolerance, mental dullness, dryness of coat and skin, excess shedding, hair thinning and even baldness.

In the face of symptoms of hypothyroidism, many vets elect to use drug therapy. Owners need to be aware of the typical signs of over-dosage with thyroxin which are twitchiness, hypo-excitability, restlessness and weight loss. If these do occur, you need to discuss with your vet whether therapy should cease or the dose should be decreased.

It is generally accepted that the cause of hypothyroidism in dogs is hereditary but there is also a theory that suggests a virus may be involved. The definitive study of hypothyroidism in dogs is yet to be concluded and may give greater insight into this condition.

74. What does a heart murmur mean for a dog?

Just like aging people, dogs can develop problems with their heart because of wear and tear. Put simply, the heart is just like a mechanical pump. It draws in blood that no longer contains oxygen, pumps it to the lungs where the red blood cells again become oxygenated, then draws the blood up into a different compartment and sends the now oxygenated blood out to feed the body.

The heart has four chambers and various valves which ensure that the blood flows in the correct directions. If one of these valves deteriorates, the blood flow is disturbed, causing abnormal pressures to occur in different regions of the body. The heart compensates for this valve failure by pumping faster, but there is only so much the pump can withstand. Increasing the heart rate is only a stop-gap measure and eventually the system will fail. This total form of degeneration is referred to as congestive heart failure.

When a dog is diagnosed with congestive heart failure through a routine physical examination and not because it is displaying any symptoms, often little needs to be done other than minimising any undue stresses on the heart. A dog that has a heart murmur because of a leaking valve should not be over-exercised or made to endure any environmental stress such as too hot or cold a climate. The dog should be fed a balanced diet that never makes it too fat.

The initial symptom of congestive heart failure is usually a decrease in exercise tolerance. What has been a normal exercise program for the dog will cause the animal to run out of puff quickly or maybe even to develop a slight bluish tinge to the tongue while panting. The order of the day is then to decrease the amount of exercise the dog is given and to arrange a veterinary examination every three to six months to establish whether or not therapy is yet required.

Eventually your dog will require therapy. The pressure will build up in various parts of the body causing changes in blood flow in the lungs and in the abdomen. When the blood pressure in the lungs builds up, the body compensates by leaking fluid outside the veins and arteries, causing the fluid to be deposited into the lung cavity. This results in the dog developing a cough. This cough is especially heard at night when the dog lies down for a while and the fluid pools in his lungs. Pressure building up in the abdomen causes fluid to be released into the tummy region, resulting in the affected animal having a pot belly. Other changes occur in all organs of the body, with the liver increasing in size and the kidneys also beginning show some signs of failure.

One of the cornerstones of therapy normally instigated early in cases of heart failure is decreasing the blood pressure with drugs. This allows better flow of blood through the lungs. At the same time, the use of diuretics encourages fluid to be removed. This will cause your dog to want to urinate far more frequently so the dose has to be correctly calibrated and administered in an attempt to maximise the benefit of the fluid tablet while not keeping the patient up all night urinating. Diuretics have the disadvantage of increasing urinary incontinence so this too will need to be discussed with your vet.

As the heart rate continues to increase, the pump becomes far too inefficient so it needs to be slowed down to allow it to empty correctly. This is achieved by using a drug called digoxin and your vet will closely monitor the dose rate as it can become toxic. The dog will be given a drug called a bronchodilator to assist in breathing and gain maximum use of the lungs that are already under stress because of fluid within them.

How long has the dog got, you ask? It varies in every case, depending upon the rate of degeneration of the heart valves. Most cardiologists believe that once drug therapy is instigated, this can assist the dog for a further two to three years but many a dog has gone well beyond that. The important issues relate to the dog's quality of life. If your dog is able to walk around, is still enjoying its food and is capable of going outside to urinate and defecate then the status quo can continue. However, when its breathing becomes so laboured and the cough so irritating that it cannot rest properly, when it finds eating a chore and has to endure continually the indignity of soiling its own bed, it may be time to consider euthanasia. See page 228.

75. What is spondylitis?

Spondylitis is a condition that affects the spine. It is an infection that enters the cartilage disc found between vertebrae disc and the bone of the adjacent vertebrae. A dog suffering with spondylitis will often have a fever, be stiff and be unable to stretch out properly when walking, and will sometimes have trouble getting up or lying down.

The fever, the lameness and the back pain are not specific symptoms of spondylitis, so the diagnosis can be difficult. Good quality X-ray images are the best aid to a proper diagnosis of spondylitis. To achieve this, the dog will have to have a general anesthetic so the spine can be carefully radiographed along its various sections, looking for areas where the bone or the disc show signs of active degeneration due to infection.

X-ray images need to be very carefully interpreted and the condition must not be confused with spondylosis, which is where stony spurs are growing off the spine. Very often spondylosis does not lead to any clinical signs and the spurs are of no consequence to the dog's health. Spondylitis on the other hand, occurs because some infectious agent has been trapped in the bone or disc and is now growing there, eating away at the tissue and causing further inflammation.

Treatment therefore has a twofold purpose. Firstly, it must attack and remove all of the infectious pathogen causing the problem; and secondly, it must relieve the pain and take away inflammation. Your vet will prescribe antibiotics as well as anti-inflammatories and painkillers. X-rays will need to be taken again after two to four weeks of commencing antibiotics to ensure that the damaged area is undergoing calcification, a sign that the damaged tissue is repairing. If this is not the case, and the area of damaged bone is becoming larger, the antibiotics will need to be changed.

Depending upon the extent of the initial lesion, your vet may suggest that antibiotics continue for a period of six months. It is very difficult for antibiotics to get effectively into every little part of the bone or disc to sterilise all the organisms involved in causing this pathology. All too often, owners stop utilising antibiotics once symptoms have abated, not realising that some of the organisms are sitting there quietly waiting for their chance to begin the process all over again. Once the antibiotic levels in the blood have diminished, the bacteria can again commence their growth and they may have developed some resistance to that particular antibiotic. This will make the next wave of spondylitis pathology more difficult to treat.

On extremely rare occasions, if the spondylitis does not respond to therapy despite having several changes of antibiotics or other anti-microbial agents, then surgery may be required. A specialist surgeon will closely examine the site, taking tissue samples to allow a definitive diagnosis and then, hopefully, therapy will be instigated. Generally, if spondylitis is treated early, actively and for a long period of time, it is usually resolved without future complications.

76. Is a hernia serious and what's the best way to treat it?

Hernias on the tummy are called umbilical hernias and occur because the muscle around belly button (the umbilicus) failed to close over when the cord that once attached the puppy to its mother shrivels up and is shed a few days after birth. The majority of umbilical hernias are of no consequence, simply entrapping a small parcel of fat, which protrudes as a bubble on the dog's tummy. Occasionally very large hernias occur in this area and vets may suggest that they need closing via surgery. These larger umbilical hernias have the potential to contain more than just fat. Usually loops of intestines are also found within the hernial sac and as these can twist, it is far better to prevent such an intestinal emergency by repairing the hernia while the animal is young and healthy.

Perineal hernias are large, usually soft swellings near the anus and they occur because of weakness followed by separation of the muscles around the pelvis. While the exact cause of muscle weakness remains unknown, several factors have been proposed. The most common of these is continued straining in chronically constipated dogs, especially males with enlarged prostates. As a result of the muscle weakness and continuous straining, some of the contents of the abdomen (the bladder, small intestines, large intestines, prostate and large deposits of fat and fluid) push their way through the muscle separation and start bulging outside the body. When one considers that such important structures are working their way outside their cavity, perineal hernias represent a potentially disastrous situation.

Continuous straining, constipation, and swelling just beside the anus are the three most consistent features of perineal hernias. Perineal hernias are most common in entire males, that is, males that still have their testicles. Because the prostate is usually involved in some way in the perineal herniation, the repair should also be accompanied with de-sexing as this quickly decreases the size of the prostate and makes it far easier for the dog to defecate. Dogs that are not castrated at the time of a perineal hernia repair have a three-times-greater chance of the herniation recurring.

After the repair has taken place, the dog should be placed on a low residue diet in an endeavour to decrease the amount of faeces. Mild laxatives can also be utilised to avoid excess straining that might otherwise occur if the faecal matter is too dry or too hard.

Perineal hernias in themselves do not present an emergency situation, but the quicker they are treated the less suffering the dog will have to endure. Also, the quicker they are treated, the less chance there is of the condition ever becoming an emergency from the complications that can arise from perineal hernias.

77. What is a pinched nerve?

The spinal column, which runs from the head right down to the tip of the tail, is made up of individual bones called vertebrae. The dog has seven of these vertebrae in the neck region, thirteen in the chest area, seven of them in the back or lumbar area, three vertebrae which are fused together in the pelvis (called the sacrum) and a variable number of vertebrae forming the tail. Their function is twofold: firstly to protect the spinal cord, and secondly to provide correct mobility of the spine so the animal can turn and function accordingly. For the spine to be able to move, each vertebra must be able to gently turn in the directions that the muscles are pulling. To achieve this for the whole column, cartilage discs between each vertebra cushion the bones against each other so that they don't clash and wear too quickly. Nerves between all vertebrae in the region of the spinal cord feed out to the body, providing the necessary neural stimulation or electrical impulses required for normal body function.

From time to time, the vertebrae may come out of absolute correct alignment and this places pressure on the nerves — it also pinches the spinal cord against either bone or muscle tissue. Similarly, the discs themselves can degenerate and when this happens the tough outer coating of the disc ruptures at the area of least resistance, which is above the disc and directly underneath the spinal cord and the nerve that is leaving the cord in the area. The inner part of the disc is made of softer material, which pushes upwards, pressing against the spinal cord and pinching the associated nerve.

In the initial stages of a degenerating disc, the dog experiences only mild pain and the condition may be treated with either anti-inflammatory therapy and rest, acupuncture or even chiropractic therapy. Prior to commencing any of these, correct diagnosis must be made otherwise the animal's hindquarter movement could be placed at great risk. Incorrect manipulation of a region that has a prolapsing disc or a cracked vertebra might result in complete and permanent hindquarter paralysis. Plain radiographs should be taken of the area to assess the degree of damage which, combined with a thorough physical examination and a neurological work up, will assist your vet in formulating the necessary therapy plan.

If the dog is in severe pain or shows signs of paralysis of the hind legs, then a specialist should be called in to perform a myelogram where dye is injected into the space between the spinal cord and the bony spinal column, and a series of X-rays determines the extent of the damage. The case should then be referred to a specialist surgeon who would remove some of the bony portions at the top of each vertebra to take pressure off the spinal cord. The alternative to this procedure is to cut a window into the bone and suck out the disc itself, but in both approaches the goal of surgery is removal of pressure from the nerve tissue.

Although any breed of dog can be affected by a pinched nerve, especially because of disc degeneration and subsequent protrusion, the condition is more commonly seen in the smaller breeds of dogs. Dogs that tend to be a bit longer in overall body length compared to their height, such as dachshund, Pekingese, basset hounds and corgis tend to suffer from a slipped disc. If you are an owner of such a dog, then you need to be well aware of the circumstances that can degenerate a disc. Avoiding lots of stairs, as well as games that can cause the dog to turn suddenly may assist in maintaining the integrity of the disc and subsequent health of the spinal cord itself.

78. Can dogs get bloat from eating grass?

Eating grass does not cause bloat in dogs. We often associate dogs eating grass with the dog being sick, but this is incorrect. Dogs commonly graze on various grasses so that they can remove excess bile from their body. See page 184 for more information.

Bloat occurs when gas or froth is trapped in the stomach. The dog is unable to empty the stomach contents into the intestines and despite repeated attempts to vomit or belch, those contents fail to be regurgitated. This trapped froth increases rapidly in volume so that the stomach begins to bulge so much the dog suffers severe pain and rapidly goes into shock.

There are many listed causes and ways to avoid bloat in dogs, but no one really knows the exact reason for this hideous condition. Because bloat can kill dogs in a matter of minutes, it is worth trying all the suggestions that might prevent the problem, especially if you own a breed that is predisposed to bloating.

The rules are:
1   Never feed a dog too soon after exercise.
2   Do not allow your dog free access to water immediately after exercise. Give a small drink then wait for the dog to cool down before allowing it to have more.
3   Try to feed your dog once the heat of the day has gone.
4   Feed in the evening rather than morning so your dog can digest its food quietly through the night.
5   Do not use food that has gone off or foods that ferment easily.
6   Avoid feeding salty or spicy food.
7   Don't feed the dog chicken bones. They can be swallowed whole, blocking the stomach exit.

Owners of deep-chested dogs such as Rhodesian ridgebacks, German shepherds, Rottweilers, wolfhounds, basset hounds, bullmastiffs, setters and a host of other breeds should be acutely aware of this problem. Many owners will keep a large sterile needle that they can plunge into the highest point of a distended stomach. This type of instant relief will not stop the disease or bloat from coming on, but it can give some momentary pain relief and allow proper breathing for a short time while staving off cardiovascular shock. In short, you can save your dog's life if you're prepared to make the plunge with the needle. It will all be to no avail, however, unless you can get the dog to a vet within a short time.

The vet will try to minimise a condition called endotoxic shock by placing the dog on intravenous fluids then administering intravenous antibiotics as well as special steroids to minimise shock. However, the blood vessels of the stomach and intestine have been severely compromised allowing bacteria and toxins from the gut to enter the dog's bloodstream. Unless these are quickly dealt with, they will cause death within 24 hours. While dealing with shock, the vet will also perform surgery to empty the stomach and possibly take corrective measures to prevent the re-occurrence of bloat. Despite all this, it is not rare for bloat to occur a second or even third time and once a dog bloats, it often eventually dies from the condition. Quick action from attentive owners affords the best opportunity to save a dog's life.

79. Why does my dog eat grass and then vomit?

In most cases where dogs eat grass and then vomit, the dog is not ill at all. Certain foods, particularly fatty or very salty meals will result in excess bile production. In humans, excess bile will simply be passed through our intestines and out in our faeces. Dogs, however, rid their body of excess bile by eating grass and after a few minutes vomiting up the grass and bile. This is evident in the thick mucus that is wrapped and intermingled with the grass, often stained yellow, indicating the presence of bile pigment.

It is up to you to observe how often this behaviour occurs and to decide if a trip to the vet is necessary. A dog that vomits more frequently than every two to three weeks and eats copious quantities of grass could be harbouring some type of parasite. In the wild, dogs will eat grass or some wild herbs in an attempt to decontaminate themselves of parasites. If your dog continually eats grass it is worthwhile having its faeces examined by a vet. Even with the most efficient of worming programs your dog can still harbour other intestinal parasites such as protozoa or bugs like giardia. It may take several faecal tests before getting evidence that a bug is present in your dog's intestines.

The investigation required for an animal that vomits too frequently depends upon the dog's history and a thorough physical examination by a veterinary surgeon. A dog that is a continuous grass-eater who frequently vomits up grass, bile and also food, may require blood tests, X-rays and possibly even an endoscopy to look inside the stomach.

Occasional vomiting of bile is not an abnormality but some owners do become concerned about it. Such dogs may benefit from a change of diet, increased vitamin content in the food or even some herbal medications. A diet low in fat, high in good quality protein and an easily digested soluble carbohydrate will be of benefit to the animal even if it's not totally necessary. The addition of B complex and other antioxidants may be beneficial in decreasing the habit of eating grass and vomiting. Finally, herbal medications may assist in breaking the habit. Saint Mary's thistle (or milk thistle) helps to stimulate metabolism and fresh garlic can assist in parasite control. Some owners have reported benefits adding a combination of cooked fresh beetroot and fresh carrot to the dog's diet.

80. What is the large fluid swelling on my dog's ear?

A diffuse swelling over the ear is usually a haematoma or blood clot. The cause is excessive scratching or shaking of the head, causing a blood vessel inside the ear flap to rupture and to leak blood between the ear cartilage and the skin. The condition is termed an aural haematoma.

Dogs will shake and scratch at their ears because of ear infections, or ear mites or a generalised allergy. Whatever the underlying cause, it too must be treated at the same time that the haematoma of the ear is treated — otherwise another haematoma can arise.

The best treatment is surgical drainage of the haematoma and stitching (suturing) the skin back down onto the cartilage. The skin will have lifted off, causing a space that is filled with blood. When the blood clots, this forms a haematoma. If the blood clot is left untreated then one of two scenarios will occur. The clot may contract, crinkling the ear flap so the dog develops a severe 'cauliflower' ear, or bacteria may grow in the haematoma, causing a severe putrefying infection, which leads to death (necrosis) of the ear flap. The infection may then spread further through the dog's system.

It is not uncommon for dogs with erect ears to have the affected ear fall down and remain so, all because of an aural haematoma. This is of no concern to the animal, but if you want to avoid this situation, you need to present a dog with a auricular haematoma to the vet within 24 hours. There's still no guarantee the ear will stand up but prompt action gives the best chance before the cartilage permanently creases.

The alternative treatment of placing a large bore needle into the haematoma to drain the region then injecting it with cortisone can sometimes be tried in patients that are a high anaesthetic risk. Results are not always favourable and surgery may need to be faced if this more conservative therapy fails.

Ear infections, mites and skin allergies can easily recur so owners need to be vigilant to ensure these problems are quickly addressed, otherwise aural haematomas can become painfully repetitive for your dog.

81. What is a 'hot spot'?

From time to time, dogs develop itchy areas on their skin. These areas may have only mild irritation, causing the dog to scratch lightly or there may be an intense irritation resulting in the dog continually scratching and chewing at the spot. The cause of the initial irritation may be a bite from a flea or an allergy to an irritant plant — in fact, the actual cause of the initial irritation does not matter. Because the irritation is so intense the animal scratches vigorously, damaging the skin and causing the area to become even further irritated. The damage to the skin also causes bacteria which normally live on the skin without causing problems, to start growing and attacking the deeper layers of the skin. This too causes further irritation and the animal responds by again scratching and chewing at the area. Chewing is particularly bad because it adds moisture from saliva to the irritated broken skin, which further promotes bacterial growth. The bacteria and the inflammation spread over this particular area and the result — you guessed it — makes the animal scratch and bite the area even further. In other words, a vicious cycle has just commenced.

This moist hot area of skin is referred to as pyoderma. 'Pyo-' is the Greek prefix which means pus, which has formed as a result of the bacterial overgrowth. The suffix 'derma' refers to the fact that the irritation is located within the dermis or skin. Severe inflammation also triggers the release of histamine into the body, causing a generalised dermatitis to occur all over the body. The poor animal's only defence now is to scratch even further on other areas and suddenly the hot spots are appearing on various areas of the skin. The bacteria continue their growth and produce gas which gives off a severe stench attracting flies to lay their eggs on the infected skin. Within less than 24 hours, maggots can be growing in the area so that the whole region becomes flyblown.

Treatment will depend entirely on the severity and spread of the symptoms. If the skin is slightly reddened, only showing signs of inflammation, then treat it with an anti-inflammatory wash, give it an extra clean with surgical alcohol or methylated spirits (which will also have a drying affect on the region) and apply a cortisone and antibiotic cream twice daily. Severe lesions may need veterinary attention which could include clipping unwanted hair from the area, washing it down with antiseptic solutions, applying various creams, as well as administering antibiotics and anti-inflammatories internally.

Hot, humid conditions are most conducive to the development of hot spots and owners need to be aware of what is occurring on their dog's skin during these climatic periods. With dogs predisposed to the condition, anti-inflammatory and antiseptic washes can be used on a weekly basis in an attempt to prevent hot spots from occurring. Diet has little to do with the development of hot spots, although ensuring the correct nutrients are available to maintain healthy skin is essential. Polyunsaturated oils, Omega 3 oils or evening primrose oil added to the diet may assist in such cases. Total prevention of hot spots is probably impossible, but if you remain diligent about meeting your dog's needs, most hot spots can be controlled.

82. What is summer itch and how do I get rid of it?

Summer itch or eczema or allergic dermatitis is very common in dogs, especially those living in warmer climates. There are also some breeds predisposed to these sorts of allergies: West Highland white terriers, some lines of German shepherds, Rottweilers, poodles and Dalmatians.

Affected dogs will often lick at their feet, rub their muzzles along the ground, chew at their back near the base of the tail or simply scratch continually, even rubbing themselves against a fence or under a table. The dog's immune system is reacting against certain substances in the environment referred to as allergens. There are literally hundreds of these that can cause a dog's immune system to overreact, releasing histamine and resulting in the dog scratching. One allergen is the saliva from fleas when they bite a dog.

More common causes are various plants – many creepers or vines are notorious for causing dogs to scratch, especially wandering jew, ivy, jasmine and morning glory. The list does not stop there. Many grasses will also cause a dog to scratch, especially buffalo, and even the new softer varieties that are supposedly more gentle. Pollens also play their role in causing allergic dermatitis in dogs so that obviously in the spring/summer months these greatly complicate the problem. Various bushes, house dust and house mites and even incorrect shampoos can all lead to generalised allergic dermatitis in dogs.

Obviously the best cure would be to remove all the allergens from the environment. However, this tends to be impossible — dogs simply cannot live in a glass bubble. Specialists can recommend a course of hyposensitisation injections that are given over a three-year period. The attempt is to continually administer tiny increments of allergens to the immune system so that that portion of the immune system eventually shuts down. It is obviously very expensive and the success rate is very low. Far less than 50 per cent of dogs that undergo this treatment appear to respond to it in clinical practice.

Antihistamines are a boost in therapy against allergies in humans but tend to be unremarkable in their actions in dogs with allergic dermatitis. The only drug that stops the release of histamine and helps in controlling allergic dermatitis appears to be cortisone. The problem is that this drug has very bad side effects if it has to be used in high doses or over a long-term period. However, used in combination with antihistamines, there is a synergistic effect: the antihistamine will have a greater than expected effect when combined with cortisone and the amount of cortisone required will be greatly reduced. Your vet will often recommend higher doses at the beginning of such a course, but then lower the dose every second or third day in order to control symptoms of dermatitis. Unlike antibiotics, where the therapy must be used absolutely as directed, cortisone and antihistamines can simply be used according to need. The goal is to utilise minimum dose for maximum effect.

This therapy should also be used in conjunction with anti-inflammatory shampoos, which assist in reducing the overall dose of cortisone required. Many such shampoos are available and it is important to find one that assists your dog, rather than being simply satisfied with whatever product you are sold in the first instance. Curing the condition is impossible but with persistence and diligent use of various drugs, allergic dermatitis can be controlled.

83. My dog has very red eyes and a discharge. Should I bath them every day with salt water?

The first thing that you need to do is to stop washing the dog's eyes with salt water. If you think about it for a moment, when you open your eyes underwater in the ocean, it does sting a little and the saltier the water, the more the stinging. As you cannot properly control the concentration of salt in the water you are bathing your dog's eyes with, it is far better to just use plain tap water. Saline is the ideal solution to wash dog's eyes with and it can be purchased from the chemist as a solution already made up in the correct concentration.

Red eyes in dogs are usually a sign of conjunctivitis. The conjunctiva is the pink membrane just on the inside of the eyelids surrounding the eyeball, both above and below. The inflammation of this is referred to as conjunctivitis. The condition in dogs usually arises because of either irritation from dust and wind or from a bacterial infection attacking the membrane. Occasionally other organisms such as viruses and chlamydia cause conjunctivitis, but these types of infections tend to be more common in cats than in dogs.

If the eye discharge is simply a grey mucus, then bacterial infection has not yet become a problem. The irritation is more likely to be due to some other physical cause. In these conditions, it is acceptable to wash the eye out frequently with warm saline and then apply something to lubricate the eye such as liquid tears or golden eye ointment. You need to ensure that this is a fresh preparation and not one that has been open for months.

If tears are continually spilling down the corners of the dog's eyes, then the tear ducts may be blocked with sand or grit, or there may be a severe inflammation. This will require veterinary intervention with

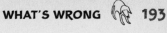

strong drugs to remove the inflammation or perhaps the animal will need to be anaesthetised so the tear ducts can be flushed.

If the discharge is yellow, then it is likely that bacteria are involved. Antibiotics may well be needed to beat the infection and cure the conjunctivitis. Your vet is the best person to decide whether these are to be used topically (an antibiotic directly on the eye), internally (tablets) or both.

Never use preparations containing cortisone without being directed by a vet. Should the conjunctivitis have resulted in an ulcer on the cornea, then applying cortisone to this will make the ulcer chronic, and could result in the cornea bursting and the eyeball shrivelling up. Cortisone is extremely powerful as an anti-inflammatory and is therefore very useful. However, its use must be restricted to specific indications.

84. My kelpie has just swallowed a golf ball whole!

I hear these stories all the time — dogs swallowing balls or other foreign objects whole, often incredibly large objects compared to the size of the dog. We even had one case at our clinic where a Doberman was presented after swallowing his owner's dentures whole. And if you think that having access to a set of false teeth is a little unusual, other swallowed items have included: Christmas baubles, waxed paper wrapping for butter, a whole apple, a shot glass full of vodka and underwear.

One item that deserves a special mention is the corncob. Dogs often enjoy chewing these after the owner has finished the corn from them, the reason being that they are usually soaked with butter. If the dog were to thoroughly chew these up, breaking them down into small pieces, they would provide a good source of fibre and fat. The problem usually occurs because the dog swallows these whole or as very large pieces. Generally, an owner is not aware of the dog's behaviour until the corn cobs turn up much later as a severe blockage. It is important to ensure that the dog does not have access to what may seen an innocuous item, but which is actually potentially lethal.

If an owner does witness a large foreign body being swallowed, immediate veterinary intervention may lead to efficient, safe and

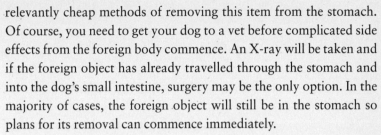

relevantly cheap methods of removing this item from the stomach. Of course, you need to get your dog to a vet before complicated side effects from the foreign body commence. An X-ray will be taken and if the foreign object has already travelled through the stomach and into the dog's small intestine, surgery may be the only option. In the majority of cases, the foreign object will still be in the stomach so plans for its removal can commence immediately.

Usually the dog will be given an emetic agent, which is a substance to make it vomit. If the object is too heavy (foreign bodies made of metal can fall into this category) or is simply located in an area of the stomach that does not evacuate, then the emetic agent may fail. Removal while it is in the stomach is always recommended as waiting for the object to pass through the intestine can meet with disastrous results. It is far easier for foreign bodies to be trapped somewhere along the intestinal tract especially where the small intestine meets the large bowel.

The simplest and most effective method of removing a foreign body from the stomach is by the use of an endoscope. This is a fibre optic device that slides down the oesophagus of an anaesthetised animal, allowing the vet to see inside. With careful manipulation, the foreign object can be located and a probe then introduced to grab the foreign object and pull it out of the stomach, up through the oesophagus and out through the mouth.

If this method is not successful, the last resort is to surgically open the abdomen and enter the stomach to remove the object. While this may seem a drastic scenario, it is far better to perform this at this time while the object is not causing any complications. Left in the stomach for any length of time, a foreign body could erode the inside lining of the stomach, causing severe damage and the possibility of endotoxic shock. A complete laparotomy without any complications would see the animal return to normal within two to four days.

85. My dog is lame in the hind leg. What's wrong?

There are no interlocking bones in the knee joint — rather the whole structure is held together by many ligaments binding bone to bone. On the inside of the knee, just at the front of the joint there are anterior cruciate ligaments. The cruciate ligaments cross from one side of the joint to the other. This X effect stabilises the joint, preventing excess rotation and stopping the lower thigh bone (tibia) from moving forward beyond the upper thigh bone (femur).

When the dog twists or turns beyond the capabilities of the tissues holding the bones, the cruciate ligaments snap. Another cause of ruptured cruciate ligaments is stopping so fast that the lower part of the limb remains firm on the ground while momentum propels the upper part of the limb forward at a jolting pace. If, usually under anaesthesia, the vet can draw the lower thigh bone forward, advancing it in front of the upper thigh, then this movement is indicative of a ruptured cruciate ligament.

A dog with a ruptured cruciate feels pain from the unstable knee every time it walks. Sometimes, anti-inflammatories may appear to relieve the pain but the relief is temporary and lameness of the affected hind leg recurs. Some owners expect a dog that is in pain to cry out. I often hear, 'He never shows any signs of pain but he's always lame.' In a dog, lameness is pain.

There is really only one effective treatment for a ruptured cruciate: surgical correction. A skilled vet will restabilise the joint by fashioning replacement ligaments using very thick suture material, the dog's own muscle in the area or both. To add to the drama of this scenario, dogs will also occasionally tear cartilages inside the joint (just like humans do!). These are inspected at the time of surgery and removed if damaged.

It all sounds complicated because it is. But if you have a dog that suddenly goes lame in a back leg it could well be a ruptured cruciate, especially if the dog fails to respond to rest and anti-inflammatory therapy. The quicker the diagnosis is made and treatment starts, the sooner your dog can be out of pain. The dog will require a rest period of about one month after surgery followed by physiotherapy.

Left untreated, the joint degenerates quickly and severely causing osteoarthritis and chronic pain. Dogs that are suffering from a 'big knee' might require major surgery to actually obliterate the joint. This is an expensive procedure where the bones of the upper and lower thigh are surgically fused. The dog remains with a limp as it can no longer flex its knee, but at least it is out of pain.

86. My dog just sliced his pad open and there's blood all over the place – help!

Don't panic. Grab a towel and wrap it around the foot keeping firm pressure on the bleeding area. Get some gauze or a pad (a woman's sanitary pad would do fine), dab some 3% hydrogen peroxide on the gauze, stick it over the dog's cut pad then wrap a bandage around the foot. Providing no blood oozes through and the bandage isn't too tight, leave the dressing on for three to six hours then gently change it. Repeat the process using the hydrogen peroxide, gauze and tape — remember, not too tight.

Most cut pads will not respond to suturing so a firm, clean dressing is sufficient to stop bleeding and protect the cut from foreign bodies such as small stones. Hydrogen peroxide (3% concentration) will assist in keeping the wound clean and will minimise bleeding. Iodine also makes an ideal antiseptic, preventing any nasty bugs that might cause infection. The wound can be initially cleaned with the peroxide after which iodine can be left on to avoid infection.

Change the dressing daily and as the cut begins to heal, the pad can be encouraged to grow out by putting mercurochrome on it twice daily to promote thickening of the black, keratinised tissue underneath.

If the cut pad will not stop bleeding, even with a dressing, then veterinary assistance will be required to suture the area down, to control haemorrhage more than anything else. Pad tissue will tend not to heal across — it needs to grow out from the soft tissues underneath.

Close inspection of a bleeding foot is needed in case the webbing between the toes is split and the pad is not cut. In this case, the webbing can be sutured, restoring the initial integrity of the foot shape.

87. My dog suddenly popped an eye out of its socket. What do I do?

Stay calm. The more you panic the harder it will be to help your dog. Get a clean towel or cloth, wet this with tap water and hold it over the eye to keep the eye moist. An ice cube on the cloth is ideal as it keeps the area damp and also decreases swelling. Now get the dog to the nearest vet.

Popping an eye out of its socket (known as a prolapsed eye) can happen to any dog if there is sufficient pressure placed behind the eye, but dogs with short noses and prominent eyes are more susceptible to prolapsing an eye. In the short-nosed breeds (brachycephalic) such as Pekingese, pugs and Japanese chins, the bony socket containing the eye is very shallow, so much less pressure is required to force the eye to pop out.

Should this occur, don't try and force the eye back into the socket as you could rupture the eyeball or cause more trauma to it. The important thing is to keep it moist so if for any reason you have no access to water, use oil, petroleum jelly or even a lubricating gel provided it is made for human use and not mechanical use.

Vets will recognise a prolapsed eye as an emergency and admit your dog immediately. Your dog will have a general anaesthetic and the eyelids may be cut open and the eyeball replaced back into the socket. Usually the area will be protected by suturing the eyelids shut while the trauma heals.

Whether sight is restored or not depends upon the amount of damage sustained to the back of the eye, where the optic nerve is attached as well as the middle section of the eye where the lens is situated. If nerve damage has occurred, little can be done. If the lens has luxated (dislocated from its normal position) a specialist could see if an attempt at re-positioning it is worthwhile. In most cases vision is lost and the eyeball is preserved for cosmetic reasons only.

The eye is treated with anti-inflammatories and antibiotics to stop swelling and prevent infection. If drainage to the eye has been affected, the eyeball will swell (glaucoma). Drugs may re-establish drainage of the eye but if the situation doesn't quickly improve, your vet will recommend removal of the eyeball as the condition is very painful.

88. What's a 'slipping kneecap' on a dog?

The kneecap (patella) is one of the three bones that make up the knee. The largest bone is called the femur and the bottom end of the femur forms the top part of the knee. The tibia, or bone of the lower thigh, forms the base of the knee. The patella sits in a groove found in the femur and slides up and down this groove to improve the function of the joint.

Dogs that have a 'slipping kneecap' have a patella that slips out of the groove of the femur. The patella slips sideways, dislocating itself out of the joint. This causes difficulty in walking and a dog with a dislocated kneecap will kick or snap the leg straight back in an attempt to click the kneecap back into the correct place. While the kneecap is outside the groove, the knee cannot function efficiently and the constant clicking in and out of the groove causes osteoarthritis.

This constant dislocation pulls the bottom attachment of the kneecap itself into an abnormal position. If you feel the sharp bit of bone under your own knee then this is the place that the ligament attaches. The constant dislocation, especially during the growing years, pulls this sharp piece of bone towards the dislocating kneecap.

Surgical repair involves firstly deepening the groove in which the patella sits and secondly, transplanting that sharp piece of bone to the proper location to ensure a straight functioning joint. Finally, the capsule around the joint is heightened, since ligaments have stretched, to prevent the kneecap from moving out of the groove.

Luxating patella, or slipping kneecap, is a heritable defect. If you are buying a puppy, especially from a small breed where the condition is more prevalent, ensure the parents have been cleared for this problem. If either the mother or father of a pup have this problem or do not have veterinary certification to prove they are clear, then look elsewhere for a pup. If you are buying a pup from a breed that can suffer from luxating patella, always have a veterinary examination to check the pup, preferably before purchase.

89. Can little dogs get hip dysplasia? What is Legg-Perthes disease?

While hip dysplasia tends to be more of a problem in larger breeds, small breeds can get it as well. However, a small dog with hip pain, especially at a young age, would more commonly reflect a disease called Legg-Perthes disease. The disease involves a process in which the ball part of the hip joint (the femoral head) and the attachment of the head to the upper thigh bone (femur) actually break up inside the body. Because the bone in this region of the hip is breaking up, the cartilage that lies on top of this bone begins to crack and collapse. As one could well imagine, this causes a great deal of pain for the animal.

Dogs with this condition are often irritable and may lick and chew their hip area in a feeble attempt to reduce their pain. The pain can be further demonstrated by gently extending the leg backwards, thereby placing pressure on the hip joint, and eliciting a pain response. The process causes severe degenerative changes in the hip joint, which, left untreated, becomes a continuously painful osteoarthritis.

X-rays show the femoral head and neck breaking up inside the body. What they do not depict is the degree of inflammation and soft tissue involvement that cause the severe pain during this type of deformity.

Conservative therapy utilising anti-inflammatory and analgesic drugs will rarely result in any relief of symptoms. The only treatment that ensures the animal can be pain-free, that stops lameness and allows the leg to return to normal function is surgical removal of the femoral head and neck. Virtually 100 per cent of animals respond to proper surgical technique as treatment for Legg-Perthes disease.

After the operation it is important that the owner forces their dog to start walking as soon as possible. Resting the dog after surgical removal of the femoral head will lead to the formation of fibrous adhesions that will minimise completely free movement of the affected leg once the muscles have healed. The best physiotherapy after a femoral head resection is long slow walks. This will be a little difficult for the dog at first as it learns to use its hind leg with a muscle sling rather than an actual joint. However, this is truly a case of no pain, no gain. Just like all physiotherapy, the process is painful but the long-term benefit cannot be underestimated.

The cause of Legg-Perthes disease is most likely genetic. Given the possibility of continuing research in this field the gene responsible might one day be located and the problem become a historical textbook entry rather than the painful disease it is.

90. Do dogs only get dysplasia in the hips?

There are three diseases that dogs can have in one or both elbows. Elbow dysplasia is one.

The three syndromes seen in the elbow joint when proper X-rays are taken are:

Osteochondroses dissecans (OCD)

This is a disease of the cartilage which can affect any joint of the body, but when the lower part of the humerus (or upper foreleg) is affected this is called elbow dysplasia. The disease causes pain and inflammation of the elbow joint which is manifested as a lameness of the foreleg. Young, growing dogs of large breeds are most commonly affected by elbow dysplasia. OCD usually results in complete remission when surgically corrected.

Un-united anconeal process

This is a large piece of bone that should knit to the ulna during the first few weeks of life. When this fails to happen, a large, loose fragment of bone rattles around in the elbow joint causing severe pain, build-up of fluid and very early osteoarthritis.

Un-united Anconeal Process was traditionally approached by removing the fragment, but the results were variable with all cases concluding with osteoarthritis. More recent attempts rely on very early diagnosis of the condition and the surgical correction involves removing a big piece of bone from the mid section of the ulna. This forces the two fragments in the elbow joint together, allowing them to unite. However, this knitting of the un-united fragment can only occur if the dog is still in the early growth phase.

Fragmented coronoid process

This is by far the hardest of the three syndromes to diagnose and treat. This component represents a tiny piece of bone fragment, smaller than half a five cent piece, but because of its location in the deepest recess of the elbow joint, it causes severe lameness.

Fragmented coronoid is the least rewarding of syndromes to treat but probably the most common. Surgical correction means aggressively opening up the elbow to remove the fragment. In many cases dogs are left just as lame after surgery as before surgery and in every case, some degree of osteoarthritis will occur because of the intrusion into the joint.

All three conditions are heritable, so buy your pup from parents that have been X-rayed and are cleared for elbow dysplasia. This is no guarantee against the disease but at least it is a good starting point. To increase your chances of buying a dog that is clear, purchase a puppy from parents that have had previous cleared litters.

Unfortunately, it is impossible to detect earlier than four to five months if a dog will develop elbow dysplasia and in most cases the diagnosis cannot be made before seven to nine months. Every case has individual facets making it essential that you be advised by an experienced vet and it may even be beneficial to seek two or more opinions.

91. What's Wobbler's syndrome?

All large breeds of dogs as well as crosses of those breeds can develop Wobbler's syndrome. The two common breeds that develop this problem are Great Danes and Dobermans.

The disease was first described in horses, and the name was based on the graphic description of the animal's hind legs wobbling around as though it was drunk. Although in scientific circles the name has changed to more technical terms, the original name, Wobbler's, is very appropriate when one sees an animal affected with this condition

The wobbling of the back legs occurs because the messages sent along the nerves from the brain to the muscles and back again are greatly disturbed or interrupted because of pressure on the spinal cord. The spinal column is a series of bones referred to as vertebrae. These bones must align themselves in a perfectly straight configuration to allow the nerve tissue, the spinal cord, to travel through them without any interruption. In Wobbler's syndrome, one or more of the vertebrae in the neck rotates and loses the correct alignment. As it rotates it squashes the spinal cord inside the restricted canal. As the rotation commences, subtle pressure on the cord disrupts its ability to send the electrical responses from the back legs up to the brain. Literally, the dog's brain doesn't know the proper placement of where its back legs should be and this causes them to wobble around. As the rotation becomes more severe, any movement of the neck can result in very severe pain. To hold their balance these animals typically develop a very wide stance and an awkward swaying movement.

Your vet can diagnose the condition by examining the clinical signs, performing a brain (neurological) assessment and radiology of the neck region. A myelogram may be needed to fully evaluate the amount of compression that is occurring in the dog's spinal column. A myelogram involves the injection of dye into the actual spinal canal and watching the movement of this dye through a series of X-rays.

Dogs that have mild to moderate signs may be treated conservatively with cortisone to decrease the inflammation in the region. While cortisone has negative side effects such as overeating, fluid retention and adrenal gland problems, patients have been managed with intermittent cortisone therapy for as long as five years. The saddest cases occur in patients that do not respond to conservative therapy. Surgical intervention can be attempted, but this is expensive and may not be successful. While some cases recover remarkably well, others, especially where the spinal cord damage is permanent, may not derive any benefit from surgical intervention, leaving the only kind alternative to finally relieve the animal from pain by euthanasia.

92. My dog just ate a packet of rat bait! What can I do?

All rat baits are based on anti-coagulants. That is, they stop the blood from clotting. Any animal, even humans, that ingests rat bait will not be able to be prevented from bleeding. Left unattended, bleeding (haemorrhaging) will occur once the poison is absorbed into the bloodstream. The bleeding will start in the intestinal system and the animal's gums will become pale. Given sufficient poison, the animal will bleed from the gums and eventually from the eyes and into the urine.

It is important to treat an animal as soon as it is known that it ingested a rat poison of any kind. If the animal has just eaten the bait, it is often possible to make it vomit to expel the poison before harmful effects begin. You are likely to require professional help but if you can't get to a vet immediately you can try a large dose of Ipecac or very salty water. A vet will be able to administer apomorphine which is a strong emetic to make the dog vomit the entire contents of the stomach.

Once the symptoms of the poison are already visible — pale gums, weakness and even bleeding — it's too late to make the dog vomit. Veterinary intervention will be necessary to save the dog's life.

Lost blood will have to be replaced by a blood transfusion. While donor blood is being located (some veterinary hospitals do not have direct access to a canine blood bank), intravenous fluids will be administered in an attempt to maintain blood pressure. However, whole blood transfusion remains the best method of saving the dog because it not only replenishes red blood cells that are essential for carrying oxygen around the body, but also gives the dog clotting factors which are desperately needed.

For the following two weeks the dog must be given maximum doses of vitamin K, a compound that helps blood clot, in case the toxin has been absorbed or is still present in the gastrointestinal tract.

93. Is snail bait dangerous?

Snail bait is even more dangerous than rodent poisons. The initial treatment, which you can only do if symptoms haven't commenced, is the same as rat bait (see page 209) — get the dog to vomit the snail bait up while the poisonous pellets are still in the stomach.

Once the pellets dissolve, releasing the chemical which is absorbed into the dog's bloodstream, then it is not only too late to make the dog vomit, it is actually dangerous to do so. Snail baits cause dogs to have a seizure. If a dog has a fit while it is vomiting the chances are that some of the vomit will go down the windpipe (or trachea), choking the dog.

A vet will anaesthetise a dog with symptoms of snail bait to control the seizures. The dog will be given the antidote (atropine), but the main two cornerstones of therapy are to keep the dog anaesthetised and to maintain a clear airway. Some dogs have been kept under a state of anaesthesia for as long as 24 hours. Intensive care and monitoring is required if any dog is to pull through a snail bait toxicity.

A word of warning when using or buying snail bait. There are products available that advertise that they are 'not attractive to dogs and cats' — in a word, baloney! If you read the fine print there is a warning that if your pet does eat it then stop using it. Oh really?

All snail baits are poisonous and all of them may be attractive to your dog to eat. If you insist on using snail bait in your garden, the pellets must be placed in an area that your dog cannot access. Otherwise, consider some other forms of snail and slug control.

94. Are all snakes venomous?

Not all snakes are venomous, but unless you're up to speed with snake identification, you should treat all snakes as if they do have deadly poison in their fangs. Remember, Australia has some of the most venomous snakes in the world, so if your dog gets bitten by a poisonous snake, quick action will be required if you're to save your friend's life.

Snake venom is divided into two categories: neurotoxin which affects the nervous system, or haemolytic toxin which affects the red blood cells. Neurotoxic poisons cause an animal to have uncontrollable tremors eventually leading to convulsions. The muscles of the diaphragm cannot contract properly causing respiratory failure and the heart muscle will quickly be affected by the severe metabolic changes due to all the muscles' involuntary contractions, causing cardiac failure. This poison is typically found in brown snakes — a dog bitten by a large brown snake can be dead in minutes.

Haemolytic poisons cause the red blood cells inside the body to simply rupture. This prevents clotting and also renders the animal critically anaemic. Dogs affected by this sort of poison will have dark or bloody urine, pale or even white gums, and will become very lethargic, culminating in a weakness that renders the animal unable to stand. They will eventually die of cardiovascular collapse. The red-bellied black snake is probably the best known example of this type of venom. While not as venomous as brown snakes, they are still deadly. The difference is that you usually have a little more time in cases of red-bellied black snake bites.

If a venomous snake does bite your dog, quick action is required. If possible, carry your dog rather than allowing it to walk. The more it exercises, the greater the circulation of venom around the body. Tourniquets are a good idea if the bite occurs on an extremity, but don't agonise over it if you don't have something suitable — the important thing is to get your dog to the closest vet.

At this time you need to realise that treatment is expensive and could amount to well over a thousand dollars. Crucial to the treatment is the use of anti-venom, and the vet will also have to instigate fluid therapy, shock prevention as well as drugs to stop allergic reactions to the anti-venom. Further, in the case of neurotoxins, the vet may need to anaesthetise the dog to control convulsions. A dog bitten by a snake that has caused severe depletion of red blood cells may need a whole blood transfusion. All these costs, plus hospitalisation fees and possible intensive care, nursing and pathology costs, can add up to a substantial account.

For those that live in a potential snake-bite area of the world, pet health insurance should be seriously considered as it will save you lots of money if your dog ever gets bitten.

Prevention of snake bite is not always feasible but a few things are worth a try. Firstly, if you live in an area where snakes do occur, keep the grass on your property short, at least around the house. Snakes don't like slithering across open ground as they become prey for their own predators, so avoid high grass or even large garden beds in close proximity to your house if you live on a bush block. Secondly, do not allow rubbish areas to build up, as these can be a good hiding place for snakes. Worse still, a snake may see such sites as an ideal location for breeding or hibernation. Thirdly, if you own poultry, keep them well away from the house or the dog. Aviaries and chicken houses invariably attract rodents and these in turn attract snakes. Keep the bird housing well raised off the ground as this goes a long way to assist rodent control. Finally, if you take your dog walking through the bush or a park where snakes have been known to occur, keep your dog on a lead. If a snake hears you coming, it's likely to slither away without you ever knowing it was in your path. Dogs rushing up and annoying or threatening a snake are the ones most likely to get bitten.

The danger months for snake bites are November (the breeding time for most snakes) and February and March (snakes are on the move, looking for somewhere to curl up for winter). While these are the dangerous months, snake bites have been recorded in Australia during every month of the year, so never be complacent about these creatures if you live near native bushland.

If you do take all the precautions and still happen upon a snake, leave it alone. Walk in the opposite direction while taking a glance back. The snake is just as frightened of you — it'll be slithering away but likely looking back at you. If a snake takes up residence around your house then contact your local council. They'll probably know of a snake relocator in the area. Remember, snakes are a protected species so if you do kill one, unless it is threatening you, then you might well be breaking the law.

95. Can dogs actually think?

Most scientists would answer this question with a simple no. The ability to reason, the capacity to rationalise, having self-awareness and possessing intelligence in order to anticipate the outcome of events are qualities that scientists believe are only retained by humans. In support of these conclusions, scientists would often cite the fact that animals were not capable of utilising tools. This of course has been rebutted because many monkeys have been witnessed utilising branches for defence or gathering of food, and birds utilising sticks to gather the foods from small crevices and many animals using rocks as hammers. Scientists in turn dispute these arguments stating they are either instinctive or learnt behaviour. If this is so, it begs the question who taught a wild monkey to pick up a stick or a rock in order to defend itself or use it in some way to gather food.

In the case of dogs and their ability to reason and to predict future outcomes, scientists can attribute neither instincts nor learning to the dogs that have pulled toddlers away from swimming pools and dams due to what can only be described as the dog's realisation that the child could die by entering the water. The water holds no fear for the dog as they can instinctively swim.

The dictionary defines reasoning as the mental powers concerned with drawing conclusions or inferences. Scientists tell us dogs do not have the power to reason. If that is the case, they are unable to reason that if there is a fire in the house they should alert the owners to ensure the safety of loved ones. Or if an owner becomes trapped by a fallen tree or in a rolled car the dog is unable to reason that it must leave its owner to find people that will assist, and even be able to take rescuers back to the site where the owner is. Yet all these things and many, many more have occurred countless times all over the world and are continually reported to the amazement of scientists who must surely question the premise that dogs are incapable of thinking.

That dogs are capable of affection, able to love and be demonstrative in doing so is beyond question. Accepting the premise that dogs are capable of love, one would also accept the fact that love is an incredibly strong motivating force. How often have you heard the words 'greater love hath no man than to give his life for a fellow human being?' Truer words have never been spoken and the same applies to our canine companions. Love for their master in the face of danger probably heightens their senses to promote their power of reasoning. Many stories are told about dogs that work in the services, either military or police. One well-documented incident occurred in Vietnam when a German shepherd, whose handler had been wounded and fell to the ground, disobeyed his conditioned training to go forward, jumping between the next volley of bullets and his beleaguered master. The dog took the hits in doing so, saving his handler's life in exchange for his own, his body falling to cover the handler. This gave sufficient time for the man's backup to arrive, return fire and make good their escape. Do dogs think like humans, conceptualising ideas? Undoubtedly the answer to that is no. Dogs are not capable of conceptualising the building of say an atom bomb, a nuclear powered missile or a hideous box filled with biological organisms that could destroy a city. In fact, dogs can't even imagine why any being would want to develop such weapons of mass destruction.

There is no doubt that dogs do not think like humans and that is probably to the canine's credit, but they think they do. When training dogs, the best trainers learn to think dog. In that way a good trainer is elevated to a non-malicious way of thinking and is capable of simpler, purer thoughts.

The whole debate as to whether dogs can think becomes clouded because of anthropomorphism — giving human qualities to animals. Many movies and television shows such as 'Lassie' and 'Rin Tin Tin' depict dogs performing acts of reason that are really only achievable by humans. A dog's perceptions and sense of values are vastly different to those of humans but this does not render them incapable of thought processes. Nor does it preclude them from some ability to have conceptual thoughts. If conceptual thinking is the utilisation of one's imagination, then daydreaming must be considered a form of conceptual thought. Since dreams during sleep are often affected by what is occurring to the subject during times of full consciousness, then night dreams are also part of the conceptual thinking process. Dogs definitely dream. With the use of electrodes attached to the skin over the scalp, scientists have demonstrated periods of brain activity in dogs similar to those of humans during dream patterns. Not needing such refined techniques as electrodes, dog owners will testify to the fact that their charges during sleep may whimper, have leg movements simulating walking or running and even bark while asleep which can only be evidence of dogs' ability to dream.

96. Do dogs see colour?

For a long time it was believed that dogs lived in a totally black and white world and could not see any colour whatsoever. This makes sense from an evolutionary point, as dogs in the wild tend to hunt in the early dawn or at late dusk. That is a time of dim light when the landscape, even to humans, is seen in mainly black and white so that brilliant colour vision is of little use.

This theory was further supported by the anatomy of the retina, a part of the eye. The retina is composed of specialised nerve cells, which receive impulses from light passing in them back to the brain as electrical activity, which allows us to see. These specialised cells are divided into two types called rods and cones. While cones are useful for colour vision, rods are utilised in dim light for black and white vision. The retinas of dogs are said to be rich in the number of rods and therefore adapted for vision in poor light. As with some other animals, dogs have a light-reflecting layer at the back of their eyes causing their eyes to shine in the dark when a torch is shone towards them. This light-reflecting layer acts to intensify the image in poor light giving them a distinct advantage during the most productive hunting times, dusk and dawn.

More recent work has established that there are sufficient numbers of cone nerve cells in a dog's eye (albeit in small numbers) that allows them to see some degree of colour. While they may not have the full degree of colour perception that humans have, dogs do have a much wider range of vision. Combined with their large number of rods a dog is able to detect even small movements over a much wider field of view. Dogs do, however, have a narrower binocular vision range than we do and are thus not as good at judging distances. This does not pose any disadvantage to a dog as they do not enjoy playing golf, but once any prey is moving the dog's eye is able to catch even the smallest of muscular movements, which is vital during a hunt.

In the dog's eyes, colour in food is not important. Smell and taste are the critical issues to a canine's palate. However, humans place great emphasis on the aesthetic appearance of food so dog food manufacturers, understanding this aspect of our nature, provide canine gourmet food that appeals to our eyes rather than the dog's. In fact, the addition of food colouring does nothing more than add unnecessary chemical waste into a dog's body.

97. Do dogs feel pain the way humans do?

Dogs feel pain every bit the way we do — old age is met with the same degenerative changes of organs and joints as humans. Consequently, old, inflamed, arthritic joints throb every bit as much in dogs as they do in humans.

Being pack animals, dogs still have those very instinctive traits deep seated within their behaviours. In a pack, a dog that cries out in pain is likely to be attacked and even killed by the other members of the pack, so their response to pain must be meted out cautiously. This is because a screaming animal will attract predators and alert prey to the presence of the pack. Nature is not interested in the survival of an individual, rather it is survival of the species that is important.

Owners are often confused about the pain their animal is suffering, and because the dog isn't whimpering they assume it is pain-free. Owners are thinking like humans instead of thinking like dogs. Humans are inclined to verbalise their pain, whereas dogs only cry out if it is an acute, sharp pain. The signs of continuous pain in a dog are lameness, slowing down, loss of appetite, seeking more warmth especially in colder weather and sometimes a desire to be left alone (not unlike humans when we're not feeling well).

There is no need for our dogs to suffer such pain in modern society. Firstly, any injury should be treated immediately and this can prevent the condition from becoming chronic. Of course, age will eventually catch up with the dog but improving an old dog's lifestyle can occur with minimal effort.

Warmth is essential, so consideration should be given to keeping old dogs indoors on cold winter nights. Bathing can avert the worry of smell but ensure you bath during the mid-morning period of warm days or at least spend some time with a blow dryer to prevent the dog getting a chill.

Medication will assist in relieving symptoms of degenerated, arthritic joints. The first stage that can be used is herbal medicine. Sea Tone, made from New Zealand green-lipped mussels is particularly useful. Celery tablets have also been utilised to relieve arthritis as well as shark cartilage and glucosamide. All these products take a while to kick in so start giving them during late summer so that they are working to maximum benefit in winter.

Non-steroidal anti-inflammatories give excellent relief in many cases without undue side effects. These products must be prescribed by a vet and used strictly as directed — gut irritation will occur if these drugs are abused. They range from old-fashioned drugs such as phenylbutazolodin through to modern products that are hitting the market place every year. The potency of each product varies so if one doesn't work for your dog, ask your vet for another one as many people have reported varying results in different cases.

As the degeneration advances it may be time to change to steroids. Cortisone is a powerful anti-inflammatory that does have side effects. Used under strict veterinary guidance, it can improve the lifestyle of old dogs for reasonable periods of time. The side effects can be kept to a minimum and the improvements in the dog certainly justify the use of cortisone during the very late stages of arthritis.

One of the most common side effects of the use of cortisone is urinary incontinence. Dogs on cortisone will leak from the bladder because they increase their water intake drastically. More medication will be needed to control the incontinence — a vicious cycle of chasing symptoms around the body is commonplace in geriatrics.

98. Do dogs feel cold the way humans do?

Winter can be a hard time on any dog but it is the very old and the very young that are most affected. Newborn puppies cannot maintain their own body temperature during the first few weeks of life so leaving bitches and their litters outside will result in high mortality rates in the puppies. Old dogs develop swollen, inflamed sore joints and winter makes these all the more painful.

The singularly most important issue in winter is warmth. Night time, especially the early hours of the morning when the temperature reaches its lowest, is the worst period. Allowing old dogs to sleep inside is fine as long as the area is warm and the dog has a soft warm bed. Insulated kennels can also work providing some form of safe heating is used. The best heating device is a heat lamp similar to the type used by farmers to raise piglets or hatch chickens. These use very little electricity and should be placed a metre or so above the dog's bed. The bed needs to be raised off the floor and should be soft and thick. With the kennel properly enclosed and insulated, this forms one of the warmest types of housing for your dog.

It is imperative that whatever your dog's sleeping arrangements are, they should be free from draughts, always dry and never susceptible to rain.

If you warm your dog with a coat, then some form of leggings need to be provided to ensure that all joints are treated kindly during the harsh winter nights.

Food needs to be adjusted during the winter months — dogs will require more calories for maintenance so increase how much you feed them. Warm broth can be poured over the dog's main meal, making it more palatable and more warming on cold winter nights.

Exercise can be difficult during winter, particularly if the owner finds it hard to leave their snug house. Dogs do need to be given some form of mental stimulation and this can occur by a few simple obedience exercises being performed inside the house or within a dry area. Old dogs benefit from some light exercise to keep their joints mobile, but if the weather does not permit this then massaging the joints with anti-arthritic preparations can assist your old friend to be comfortable during cold periods.

Many old dogs will eventually become unresponsive to therapy during very cold winters. If you can't maintain your pet's quality of life, you may need to discuss the option of euthanasia with your vet.

99. How can I deal with incontinence in my old dog?

Urinary incontinence in dogs is not uncommon as they grow older. This is especially true of de-sexed females and it can occur as early as six years of age. It is vital you seek help — left untreated, a bitch with urinary incontinence will quickly develop cystitis, as there is a wet track for bacteria to travel up from the outside into the bladder. From there, bacteria will continue to colonise further up into the kidneys causing nephritis. Consequently, the need to aggressively treat urinary incontinence becomes paramount as the problem itself leads to such horrendous complications such as kidney failure.

The most common reason why female dogs develop urinary incontinence is lack of hormones, especially oestrogen. In de-sexing a female dog, the uterus and the ovaries are removed thereby depriving the animal's body of the benefits of the hormones oestrogen and progesterone. The removal of hormones leads to atrophy of the vulva and vagina that is often manifested by the inability to hold urine within the bladder. It trickles out slowly without conscious knowledge of what is occurring. Hence, incontinence during sleep occurs often in older de-sexed bitches.

Treatment of hormonal incontinence is relatively easy with the use of hormone replacement therapy. Oestrogen administered once or twice weekly is usually sufficient to attain a positive response for hormonal urinary incontinence. There are some concerns that this drug causes cancer and anaemia, but the low doses make the danger minimal and the benefits far outweigh any risks.

In castrated males, urinary incontinence can occur because of lack of testosterone. Hormone replacement therapy in these cases can be beneficial and testosterone as either monthly injections or twice weekly tablets can assist in the dog regaining control of its bladder function.

Not all cases of urinary incontinence are due to a lack of hormones. Your vet will need to exclude other disease processes that can lead to your animal dribbling urine. Simple infection of the bladder (cystitis) needs to ruled out as a possible cause. Your vet will send a sample of urine for culture to see if any nasty bugs are growing inside your dog, causing inflammation of the bladder.

Another common cause of incontinence is bladder stones (urinary calculi). The majority of these can be diagnosed by an X-ray although one type is transparent to normal X-ray techniques. Fortunately, this last type is rare and are mainly seen in Dalmatians. If stones are found in your dog's bladder, it will require surgery in the first instance to remove them and then dietary management to avoid their recurrence.

The filling and emptying of the bladder is controlled by the nervous system. Some nerve impulses come direct from the brain while others occur as a result of spinal reflexes which, in the case of the bladder are centred around the lower back. Damage or degeneration from arthritis of this spinal column can lead to improper control of urination, and the dog developing urinary incontinence because of poor nerve control (neurogenic bladder). These cases are far more difficult to manage. Early cases may respond to pseudoephedrine, an antihistamine, which does have some action on the nervous system.

The main problem with the neurogenic bladder is that the dog fills the bladder totally but fails to control its emptying. Hence the bladder simply overflows, continually causing all the problems associated with chronic incontinence.

Your vet will endeavour to suggest appropriate pharmacological management or teach you how to express the bladder for your dog. The issue of a neurogenic bladder is very complex and requires patience on the part of the owner and persistence on the part of the vet to try all avenues of therapy in an effort to manage the problem.

100. Do dogs go senile?

Although senility in animals has not been widely studied, people who work and live with dogs over a long period of time can testify to the fact that senility seems to affect dogs. One man who worked in this field has described a problem in geriatric dogs called canine cognitive disfunction syndrome. Dogs that suffer from this syndrome are characterised by decreased interest in their environment and a decreased ability to interact correctly with humans and other animals.

You should realise that the family pet might become more aggressive when it reaches senility. Various treatments have been tried in order to assist with the overall mental problems seen in older dogs and some can improve their moods. You need to learn to compensate by doing such things as ensuring the dog has a warm, comfortable space where it can lie and sleep undisturbed, especially by youngsters. Having been your friend for over ten years, serving you by guarding your life and property, your dog does deserve its space and comforts during the twilight years of its life.

101. How do I know if it's the right time to put my dog to sleep?

Often people bring their old dogs to see me and ask the question, 'How will I know when it's the right time?' My answer is nearly always the same. I simply tell people because they care enough to make such an enquiry for the one you love, they will know in their heart when the time is right.

There are, of course, certain signs. If your dog can get up to eat and drink, can go outside to the toilet, can still recognise your return from work or shopping, then all is well even if they spend most of their time sleeping. When they do not go outside to relieve themselves, have trouble standing to eat or drink, or have become so senile that they snap at every person — then it is time to let them go. Dogs become embarrassed the way you and I would, so we shouldn't let them lose their dignity.

Urinary incontinence can occur because of hormonal or even infectious reasons, so this needs to be discussed with and treated by your vet. There are many useful drugs that can improve the quality of life for a geriatric dog. Never be shy about asking your vet for assistance as, like older people, checkups by the doctor shouldn't be left until the condition becomes serious. Caught early, many geriatric conditions can be treated, extending your dog's life expectancy while maintaining good quality of life. But this therapy must not be pushed to the very extreme, as there comes a time when drugs and any other areas you might have explored no longer help.

The other matter that needs to be addressed is the issue of how the act of euthanasia (putting your dog to sleep) will be performed. Will it be painful?

An intravenous injection is used, a compound called phenobarbitone, a general anaesthetic. The dog is taken into a state of deep sleep, the anaesthetic effect continuing until heart function is also anaesthetised. The heart stops, circulation around the body ceases and in less time than it takes for you to remove a tissue from your pocket, the dog has passed on, peacefully and painlessly.

At times, people are left wondering if it is the right time because the dog was not constantly whimpering in pain but dogs just don't do that. The signs of pain are the inability to walk, lameness, loss of appetite, lethargy and often, mental dullness. One needs to assess the quality of life that the pet is maintaining or rather, in cases of pain, enduring.

There are no fixed rules or formulas to help make your decision as to when is the right time. Use common sense, don't allow your dog to suffer or lose its dignity, and listen to your heart. You will know when the time has come to accept your greatest and final responsibility as a dog owner — saying goodbye to an old friend.

Acknowledgements

Trying to produce concise, accessible information on sometimes very technical topics means lots of input from lots of people. Thankfully, my wife Fiona was always there to listen to some of the garbled words I wrote, directing me immediately back to the initial draft for changes. So many of my friends assisted too, not the least of whom was Lynn Butler, reading through the first draft and making constructive suggestions.

To Mark and Garry Lester, life-time school friends, for their introduction to my book agent, Bruce Kennedy who encouraged me and found just the right publisher, thank you. Writers are known for their tardiness, but Cassandra Booth kept me working, with her constant demand for more words to type allowing me to come close to deadlines.

The first time I heard Sue Hines's voice, I knew she would be the person to publish my inaugural book. Sue has completed this feat with great professionalism and with great backup staff in the form of the person I now call my patient and persistent friend, Andrea McNamara. You have made this a far better effort than I would have on my own and I owe you my eternal thanks for the things you have both taught me.

Finally, to my dogs. Thank you for being there, ever-ready to just love me and listen to me pour out my heart. You have heard all my secrets and never once divulged them to anyone.

Index